CHANNEL DASH

The Drama of Twenty-four Hours of War

Terence Robertson

CHANNEL DASH

Published by Sapere Books.

24 Trafalgar Road, Ilkley, LS29 8HH

United Kingdom

saperebooks.com

ISBN: 978-1-80055-835-9.

TABLE OF CONTENTS

1588

"Whomsoever shall challenge our right to call this channel English shall founder upon his own misjudgment."

Sir Francis Drake, after the defeat of the Spanish Armada.

1942

"Our passage through the Straits of Dover, the most critical point on our route, was no more difficult than an exercise in home waters."

Vice-Admiral Ciliax, German commander of the Channel Dash squadron

1942

"Why?"

Sir Winston Churchill, at the end of the day.

PROLOGUE

At the outset of 1941, Germany's fast, heavy-gunned 30,000-ton battle cruisers, *Scharnhorst* and *Gneisenau*, evaded the Home Fleet's northern patrols and broke through the Denmark Strait into the Atlantic. For the next two months they emerged from the wild Atlantic hinterland to make spasmodic raids on our shipping lanes.

The two warships had sunk more than twenty ships totalling some 100,000 tons when, in late February, 1941, they vanished from sight.

Their disappearance into the seldom-sailed tracts of the ocean deepfield caused anxious staff officers at the Admiralty in London to thin down the Mediterranean and Home Fleets and provide a battle squadron to cover our convoy routes. At the same time the depleted Home Fleet had to be maintained at Scapa Flow to guard against the new enemy battleships, *Bismarck* and *Tirpitz*, making a similar breakout from Norwegian bases.

During March there was a lull in raider operations. The battle cruisers gave no sign of their whereabouts, and the Admiralty focused attention on the Indian Ocean, where only light forces were maintained, but across which large convoys were sailed to build up our eastern defences against the threat of a glowering Japan.

As the winter days flicked by, the Royal Navy waited impatiently for the enemy ships to give some indication of life. Hastily organised cruiser patrols in the Indian Ocean and South Atlantic maintained radio silence. There was nothing to report.

Where were the *Scharnhorst* and *Gneisenau*?

To the man cycling hurriedly along country roads on a dark March night it seemed likely that his news might well weigh heavily on the scales of war. His composed expression and air of calm weariness gave little sign of the excitement within him as he drew nearer to his destination — a secluded farmhouse, five miles from Brest.

Once — and it was infinitely long ago — he had been a Lieutenant-Commander in the French Navy; now he was a dockyard fitter working for the German Navy, which occupied the port. He was also a British agent.

He reached the farmhouse well before midnight. The farmer was already in bed, but his wife greeted their visitor warmly with an invitation to stay for supper. Her daughter, smiling coyly, led the man to a settee, where they sat close together. If the unseen eyes of the Gestapo had been watching to see what a tired dockyard fitter was doing by riding five miles after a long day's work, even they might have melted at this scene of courtship.

After sufficient time had passed to convince any "shadow", the couple rose from the settee and went down some stairs to the basement. There, among rotting vegetables, rusting farm equipment and cast-out furniture they dropped the romantic charade.

While the man lit a cigarette and paced the floor, the girl produced a tiny box containing a wireless transmitter. She clipped a wire to another leading from the ordinary aerial upstairs and muttered:

"Ready."

Like the former French naval officer, this farmer's daughter had become a British secret agent.

Slowly, so that the girl would have time to translate his words mentally into code, the man dictated a brief message to London — a message which was to end the long weeks of waiting at the Admiralty. It took little more than a minute, long enough when radio detector vans patrolled the area constantly, before the transmitter was returned to its hiding-place and the couple climbed upstairs arm in arm, as befits young lovers.

Their good-night embrace later was warm, sincerely warm, as the man expressed his silent gratitude that she should have helped so bravely to send his important information to London. As a naval expert he realised how vital it was that the Admiralty should know that, but a few hours before, the *Scharnhorst* and *Gneisenau* had arrived in Brest. Imperative now to transmit the news of their departure.

At 11 am on Monday, February 16th, 1942, five men met in London to open the first and only judicial inquiry into the conduct of a battle. It was drearily dull, with persistent drizzle adding to the misery of a winter day in wartime. Inside a corner room on the first floor of the Admiralty overlooking Horse Guards Parade the pretence of a coal fire permitted by fuel-economy regulations gave little warmth. Instead the room soon became smoky and the five faces glowed pallidly in the reflection of naked lights from barren, cream-painted walls — a grim, starkly bare setting for a Board of Inquiry.

The Naval Secretary to their Lordships of the Admiralty had prepared the scene in advance with a memorandum to Mr C. T. M. Waldock of the Administrative Branch which said:

> The Whitehall Room is allocated to the Board of Inquiry to be presided over by Mr Justice Bucknill from Monday, February 16th. Pens, pencils, blotting paper, scribbling pads, foolscap sheets and water-bottles with glasses are to be

provided. Mr Waldock will see that a responsible Established messenger is in attendance.

Mr Waldock sat now with his opposite number from the Air Ministry, Mr M. J. Dean, behind a scarred, ink-spattered table to the left of the door. They were the official Secretaries to the Board. To their right and end-on to the door was the long desk behind which sat the three members of the Board — nearest the door, Air Chief Marshal Sir Edgar Ludlow-Hewitt, Inspector-General of the Royal Air Force and the Air member; to his right sat the president, Mr Justice Bucknill; on the extreme right and furthest from the door sat the Naval member, Vice-Admiral Sir Hugh Binney.[1] The be-medalled dark and light blue uniforms of the two Service officers provided the only relief in the otherwise forbidding, cheerless room in which, even though it was morning, the blackout curtains had been tightly drawn.

About six paces across the room, against the facing wall, was a row of three chairs reserved for witnesses — six paces which, in the coming days, might be the narrow gap separating men from their careers.

In an outer room the witnesses would wait their turn to give evidence in the stern presence of an armed Royal Marine sentry. The "Established" messenger sat behind a table near the door.

Mr Justice Bucknill picked up a slip of paper and read aloud:

"On the instructions of His Majesty's Government a Board of Inquiry is appointed consisting of Mr Justice Bucknill assisted by Vice-Admiral Sir Hugh Binney and Air Chief Marshal Sir Edgar Ludlow-Hewitt."

---

[1] Mr. Justice Bucknill and Admiral Binney have since died. Sir Edgar is retired.

He paused to glance at the officers sitting on his left and right. The Admiral was a comfortable-looking person, almost portly. Quick, bright eyes roved constantly with the anxious look of a mother caring for her brood. Sir Edgar, one of the tallest men in the Royal Air Force, was by contrast leanly athletic with hard, piercing blue eyes set deep in a tanned, rugged face. Between them, Mr Justice Bucknill had the delicate, gaunt, slightly regal air of an experienced judge and advocate. He continued:

"The Board's terms of reference are to inquire into the circumstances in which the German battle cruisers *Scharnhorst* and *Gneisenau*, in company with the heavy cruiser *Prinz Eugen*, proceeded from Brest to Germany on February 12th, 1942, and on the operations undertaken to prevent them."

The Judge hesitated again and adjusted his glasses. "The terms of reference," he concluded, "are signed by Winston S. Churchill, Minister of Defence."

Eleven months had passed since the French dockyard fitter informed the Admiralty that the *Scharnhorst* and *Gneisenau* had reached the comparative safety of Brest. From that moment plans had been made in co-operation with the Air Ministry for turning the Brest refuge into a trap. But in those eleven intervening months something had gone wrong. Only four days before the Board of Inquiry sat in the Whitehall Room, the ships had broken out of Brest, dashed up Channel and reached the sanctuary of home waters — the most powerful enemy battle fleet afloat had openly flouted the Royal Navy's supremacy in the Channel and passed unscathed through the Dover Straits.

The nation was angry and indignant at this affront to British prestige; there was a deep sense of shock and amazement that for the first time in nearly 300 years enemy ships had sailed within 18 miles of the English south coast.[2] There was also an insidious suspicion that, at a time when the war was not going well on land, the enemy might also prove supreme at sea.

Three days later the fall of Singapore had led to the capture of 100,000 British and Imperial troops. But this disaster caused only a ripple on the surface of national feelings already absorbed by the impudent boldness and apparent success of the German fleet.

In the Commons it was said that February 12th, 1942, saw the "War's greatest blunder" and *The Times* gave voice to public anger in an editorial:

> Vice-Admiral Ciliax has succeeded where the Duke of Medina Sidonia failed. Nothing more mortifying to the pride of sea power has happened since the 17th century.

It was this powerful pressure of national bitterness which had forced the Government to set up the Board of Inquiry. Now it was the task of the three men at the Admiralty to find out the facts. What had gone wrong and why?

The witnesses to be called would range from Air Marshals and Flight Sergeants to Admirals and Able Seamen. Each in his turn would sit in one of the three chairs facing the Board and tell a part of the story, until finally the whole series of events which led up to, and took place on, February 12th would unfold before the Board. A nation bred to believe in the invincibility of the Royal Navy, in the indomitable spirit of the RAF, demanded an explanation. The findings of the Board would have to be uncompromising and solid.

For the next fifteen days these three men would glimpse in the terse accounts of sailors and airmen something of the

---

[2] In 1690 a French fleet commanded by Admiral Tourville defeated an Anglo-Dutch force off the Isle of Wight.

savagery, something of the ferocity, with which the most concentrated and vicious sea battle of the war was fought out in the swirling mists of the Narrow Sea. They would hear a Fleet Air Arm pilot who survived mutter twice at the conclusion of his evidence:

"It was awful."

CHAPTER 1: THE MAN FROM TIPPERARY

U-boats blazed trails of wreckage across the Atlantic; it needed but a little extra effort by the enemy at sea, and Britain, alone and barely sustained by semi-belligerent America, might be forced to yield for want of ships.

At the Admiralty there were no illusions about the form this additional effort would take. From Brest the great battle cruisers *Scharnhorst* and *Gneisenau* could strike at our already badly-mauled convoys in the North and South Atlantic. If *Bismarck* and *Tirpitz* — even one of them — could slip up to Norway and then run the gauntlet through the Denmark Straits, Germany's raider power in the open seas would suffice to finish the job started by the U-boats.

Both London and Berlin were acutely aware of this. The initiative lay with the German Navy; our survival depended on our ability to seek out and destroy the enemy should he sail. Moves were made by both sides almost simultaneously.

In April, 1941, the Royal Navy and Royal Air Force corked the Channel at Dover with what were called "Channel Stop" forces. These consisted of a Blenheim bomber squadron based at Manston, Kent, which would co-operate with Fighter Command and the Dover light naval forces in shipping strikes against enemy convoys passing through the Straits by night as well as by day. It was thought that this might also discourage any German attempts to send large naval forces westwards through the Channel.

The Dover naval forces consisted of a few motor torpedo boats, it being considered unwise to maintain larger warships any closer to the German Air Force than the Scottish ports.

Then the German Navy exploited their strategic advantage. *Bismarck*, accompanied by the heavy cruiser *Prinz Eugen*, sailed from Bergen by night and vanished into the northern sea wastes. On May 21st Coastal Command reconnaissance aircraft confirmed that she had left harbour. By noon the news had reached Whitehall — the *Bismarck* was out.

Next morning the Home Fleet, with the new aircraft carrier *Victorious*, sailed from Scapa Flow and raced to intercept the enemy ships south of the Denmark Straits. On the 23rd the enemy was sighted by the cruisers *Suffolk* and *Norfolk*, then patrolling the Straits. They shadowed *Bismarck* and *Prinz Eugen* throughout the night, and at dawn the enemy were brought to action by the veteran battle cruiser *Hood*, and the brand-new battleship *Prince of Wales*, at sea on her maiden voyage. *Hood* was sunk and *Prince of Wales* so badly damaged she took no further part in the fight. The chase went on.

Although steaming at 27 knots, the Home Fleet had little hope of making a successful interception unless the *Bismarck*'s speed could be drastically reduced. That afternoon the *Victorious* was detached with orders to proceed independently to within aircraft-striking distance of the enemy.

On the wet, slippery flight deck a squadron of Swordfish torpedo bombers warmed up, waiting for the orders to take off. Large, cumbersome biplanes, they looked like relics of an earlier war as they were taxied into take-off positions. In the first plane was the leader, Lieutenant-Commander Eugene Esmonde, one of the most experienced pilots in Britain and the man the Navy counted on to avenge the sinking of the *Hood*. It was pertinent that the man on whom so much rested at that critical moment was the product of a family who for generations had been in the van of another fight, the struggle for Irish freedom.

Who was this Esmonde?

His boyhood was spent at Drominagh, a great Georgian mansion, rising high above the tranquil, heavily wooded banks of Lough Derg, in lovely Tipperary.

From a distance the dense foliage of the elms and beeches seems to embrace the grey-painted walls; from the nearness of its gardens those same walls are friendly, beckoning to the stranger to enter and enjoy warm hospitality.

Drominagh is a symbol of bygone Irish feudalism. Gracious, aloof, dominating and arrogant, it commands a countryside of indescribable beauty, with woodlands and pastures running down to the shores of the lake.

Today it carries age heavily, and centuries of sun and storm have weathered its face. Yet not so long ago the splendid, haughty rooms and thickly carpeted corridors resounded to the laughter, and absorbed the sorrows, of Ireland's great Norman Roman Catholic family, the Esmondes.

Bred of the Normans who long ago became "more Irish than the Irish", the Esmondes have never wavered from their allegiance to Roman Catholicism, a fine and deeply embedded sense of duty and the political purpose of throwing the English out of Ireland.

Since the war the family have left Drominagh and spread their influence across the world. The house by the shores of Lough Derg lives with them still — there can be no story of the family without Drominagh.

The Esmondes are a family of contradictions. Dr John Esmonde, father of two broods, one born in the late eighteen hundreds, and a second in the early nineteen hundreds, was a fervent Irish nationalist and a member of the great John Redmond's Home Rule Party in the House of Commons. Drominagh echoed when he enthralled his children with rehearsals of speeches consigning all Englishmen to the devil and placing his own countrymen on the right hand of God.

Yet the walls of Drominagh's magnificent drawing-room carried symbols of another tradition. There was hung the portrait of Colonel Thomas Esmonde, one of the first recipients of the Victoria Cross, won in the Crimea for "repeatedly rescuing wounded under fire of shell and grape shot and particularly for extinguishing a fireball before it could betray the position of his men". He rolled his body over the ball until the fuse was snuffed out.

Beside this picture was another, this one of an earlier John Esmonde who was hanged by the British in 1798.

Paradoxically, next to this picture was one of the hanged man's son, who, despite his father's unfortunate fate at the hands of the English, joined the Royal Navy and eventually became captain of the frigate *Lion*, first British warship to bear this distinguished name.

Dr Esmonde had three sons by his first marriage, the elder inheriting an ancient Wexford baronetcy to become Sir John. On another wall at Drominagh was framed the letter sent by King George V to the parents of all who fell in the Great War. Dr Esmonde's younger son, Geoffrey, had died on the battlefield at Ypres serving with the British Army. There were also three daughters by this marriage. Their mother died at the turn of the century, and Dr Esmonde married his second wife, Eiley, who bore him a girl and six boys, among them Eugene.

In the family tradition, the half brothers and sisters were taught to believe in their religion; a high sense of responsibility

and patriotism; and in the performance of duty no matter what
the cost.

They inherited the richest country life in the world. They
grew up on a lakeside where great flights of duck, wild geese
and sometimes a white armada of swans came in low to the
shore from across water of constantly changing colour.

All that could be learned of the ways of birds and fish, wind
and water, they were taught by the ageing steward and
gardener, Danny, and his son, Jack, who shot and rode with
the best of them. And when childhood and boyhood gave way
to manhood each of the sons carried with him the love of
peace and home, the knowledge that the only true way to fly is
like the birds — nose into the wind.

When the time came for each in turn to make his way in the
world, they carried with them the memory of a great grey
house, dreaming in the coloured loveliness of strikingly green
fields, with the purple Tipperary mountains in the background,
like some brooding mother waiting to welcome them home
again.

It was Eugene who travelled furthest. Educated by the
Jesuits at Wimbledon College and at Clongowes Wood in
Ireland, he went later to the Mill Hill Fathers at St Peter's
College, Freshfield, to test his vocation for the foreign
missionary priesthood.

About the only point of agreement between Eugene and the
Fathers was on his unsuitability for missionary work. It was an
odd choice of career from the beginning. Small and wiry — he
was only five feet six — with a round face and bright, alive
eyes, he was a strange mixture of mischievous fun,
intellectualism, sober-mindedness and native shrewdness. It
was, perhaps, the inborn love of space which had made him
yearn for a life in some uncivilised community.

He parted with the Fathers on excellent terms and promptly decided on a more civilised and thoroughly dangerous method of finding room to breathe — the air. In 1928 he joined the Royal Air Force with a short service commission, at once volunteering to take part in bomber operations over the sea, a decidedly risky affair not many of those early pioneers cared to chance. There was no Fleet Air Arm in those days, and although the Navy operated several aircraft carriers, the first biplane bombers attached to them were manned by the RAF.

Landing these ancient Wellesley bombers on the tiny floating flight decks then in fashion was not considered a pastime to be undertaken lightly. But the risks were almost non-existent to Eugene Esmonde, who flew because he loved flying, and stunted because he always knew the limits to which his aeroplane could be driven.

The Wellesleys were limited in range, and after a year Eugene became bored. There were too many countries to be explored and too much space untouched for him to be entirely happy with the confined quarters of aircraft carriers. His opportunity to change came when Imperial Airways, forerunner of BOAC and pioneer of the Australia route, announced its plans for expansion.

By 1933 the Company had established routes to India and beyond to Rangoon. They planned to take in Singapore and extend the service as far as Darwin, in Northern Australia. Such far-sighted policy needed pilots to put it into effect; not carefree youngsters, but experienced men with a sense of responsibility and the patience to endure long hours in the air while remaining constantly alert to the safety of passengers.

In all Eugene's training and final maturing as a pilot even his most reckless moments had been tinged with careful assessment of the odds. This had been noted in his confidential records and was to stand him in good stead when he applied to Imperial Airways for a job. He was accepted, and left the RAF with some regret but excited at the future.

The adventurous spirit nurtured at Drominagh quickly found ample scope for expression. It was an age when imaginations had been captured by the possibilities envisaged in commercial flight. For the next five years young Eugene Esmonde, then twenty-three, was to play an active and major role in the turning of those visions into reality.

By 1936 he ranked high on the list of experienced pilots, then almost all employed by Imperial Airways. His co-pilots referred to him as the "smallest meteor alive". He was never conscious of his lack of inches; his vital personality made it almost unnoticeable to others. If a friend made jocular reference to it, he would reply: "Yes, but if the engines pack up you need a parachute. All I need is a pocket handkerchief."

He delivered the first internal air mails in India to the Viceroy and his wife, Lord and Lady Linlithgow. And in the meantime others of the Drominagh brood were spreading their wings. Witham Esmonde had joined the Royal Navy as an engineer officer, first of this generation to take permanent service under the British Crown. Eugene's twin brother James had qualified as a mining engineer and had taken up an appointment in the Gold Coast. The careers of all three were to meet when the fate of Britain lay in the war at sea.

Hitler's rantings reached a crescendo at the Nuremburg Rally in 1938 and the paradox in the Esmondes came out again in Eugene. While politically he was anti-English and spiritually he was anti-war, he could permit no foreigner to malign Britain; the foreigner in question was undoubtedly anti-Christ and therefore opposed to Roman Catholicism. With these differences of principle resolved, his next problem was to decide whether at this stage he could afford to give up a good salary from Imperial Airways in return for a dubious future in one of His Majesty's armed forces.

In January, 1939, the solution to his troubles came from the Admiralty. The Navy had formed the Fleet Air Arm some years earlier, but lacked trained pilots to give it backbone. Eugene had been brought up on the flight deck of carriers, and his name was recalled by those responsible for this young branch of the Navy. A letter was sent to him care of Imperial Airways which said:

> There is an urgent need in the Air Branch for pilots with your qualifications. It is suggested therefore that you should consider a commission in the Fleet Air Arm which would mean your appointment to a position of responsibility.

Being prepared to nibble but not yet bite, he replied:

> I am interested in your offer of a commission in the Fleet Air Arm. Before giving it serious consideration I should like clarification of the following:
> 1. With what rank shall I be commissioned?
> 2. Will I be eligible for pension and if so, after what length of service?

This last point had become important to Eugene and Drominagh. His father had died and his mother was maintaining the great house on a comparatively small income. It was his wish to share in the running costs.

The Admiralty offered a commission as lieutenant-commander, guaranteed service of at least fifteen years and retirement on a pension. For a man of thirty this was a reasonable prospect.

With puckish whimsy, he sent another letter asking:

> Does the guarantee of fifteen years service at least, prevent
> me from becoming an admiral?

The Secretary to the Board of Admiralty replied in similar
vein:

> Not at all. If you elect to remain in the Service you might well
> become an admiral if that is really what you want.

The implied humour amused Eugene. He accepted by return
of post.

In April Lieutenant-Commander Eugene Esmonde reported
for duty, one rank senior to his elder brother Witham, who had
joined nearly fourteen years before. He was sent to Lee-on-
Solent, the Fleet Air Arm's base near Portsmouth, to take
command of a Swordfish training squadron. These great
single-engined biplanes were the Service's only torpedo
bombers at the time. Built of wood and light metal struts on
which fabric fuselage was drawn tightly across to form the only
protection, they resembled First World War bombers with
open cockpits. The Swordfish had three — the pilot's in front
behind the engine cowling, then the observer's, while in the
rear was the gunner's cockpit with a machine-gun on a swivel
mounting. Yet these aircraft had an important advantage over
their modern sister aircraft. They could absorb tremendous
punishment. Anti-aircraft shells passed through the fabric
instead of exploding against it, as they would against metal
fuselage. It remained, however, lamentably true that with a top
speed of only 90 knots, the Swordfish could almost be plucked
from the air by gunners.

With Witham and Eugene in the Navy, it would be logical to
expect an Irish nationalist family to consider that two sons too
many were fighting for England. But logic had little in

common with the Esmondes — or perhaps too much — when they felt stubborn. Owen Esmonde, eldest son of the second family, took a commission in the RAF and Patrick, inevitably called Paddy, qualified as a doctor and promptly joined the Royal Army Medical Corps. In the Gold Coast, James was among the first volunteers for the Home Guard while their sister Carmel joined the WRAF.

During 1940 Esmonde acquired the nickname "Winkle" — not even he was entirely sure of its origin — and served in the carriers *Victorious* and *Furious*. While in the latter he found a new sense of vocation.

"I can think of no greater honour," he wrote home, "nor a better way of passing into Eternity than in the cause for which the Allies are fighting this war."

To symbolise this spirit of dedication, he painted a free and unfettered Crusader's head on the nose of his Swordfish. The Irish nationalist could say what he pleased about the English. That was a family quarrel; the German must die for his insolence.

In the spring of 1941 Esmonde took his squadron back to *Victorious* while the web of events spread to enmesh, and then thrust, him into the foreground of battle.

In the high latitude south of the Denmark Strait sunset was not until an hour after midnight, so it was still light when Eugene Esmonde led his squadron of Swordfish into the air to avenge the *Hood*.

The weather was showery, but between squalls visibility was good. At 11.30 pm, when 120 miles from the carrier, Esmonde's striking force sighted *Bismarck*. They circled to attack from ahead, but lost contact in drifting cloud. Esmonde broke into the clear over the cruiser *Norfolk*, which signalled that the enemy was steaming to the north-west.

The squadron entered cloud again and some minutes later emerged from a black squall to find themselves over a United States coastguard cutter. At the same time the enemy, more than six miles away, sighted the squadron and opened fire with heavy anti-aircraft guns.

As the Swordfish closed the target, short-range weapons opened fire and the lumbering biplanes were caught in a barrage from both enemy ships.

Esmonde was in the lead and still four miles away when his aircraft leapt upwards, momentarily out of control. He had been hit. Fighting the controls, he steadied the Swordfish and aimed the nose at *Bismarck*. Beneath the fuselage the long, unwieldy torpedo shook in the grips as the aircraft reached a vibrating 85 knots.

They drew close to the port beam and Esmonde signalled the sub-flight behind that he intended swerving across the enemy bows to attack from the starboard side. But the antiaircraft fire was too deadly; he changed his mind and maintained course.

At less than 1000 yards and at little more than 100 feet above the sea, Esmonde's first sub-flight let go their torpedoes and banked away. The next two flights, not satisfied with their approach runs, came in again from different directions, fired their torpedoes and turned to rejoin Esmonde, who was leading his planes up and down the line of attack in an attempt to draw off the heavier gunfire.

Suddenly there was a dull roar, followed by a flash and huge plume of smoke, and spray belched from the *Bismarck*, She had been hit amidships. Esmonde signalled *Victorious*:

Have attacked with torpedoes. Only one observed.

The squadron was not yet out of danger. The carrier had altered course while the aircraft had been away and there was no sure way of finding her. Yet they did, but as they came in to land, a violent squall struck, blotting out the sea. The carrier switched on searchlights, and with their glare in the dense rainstorm acting as a guide, the Swordfish were brought into land.

Esmonde and his crews had cause for celebration that night. They had not sunk the battleship, but had seemingly accomplished their mission and reduced the speed of the enemy. According to textbooks they should have been shot to pieces.

It was enough. Three days later the Home Fleet brought the *Bismarck* to action and destroyed her.[3] Only four hours before this attack the *Prinz Eugen* was able to slip away unseen and make good her escape to Brest.

In his report to the Admiralty, the Commander-in-Chief, Vice-Admiral Sir John Tovey, said:

"The attack by the Swordfish squadron so lately embarked in a new carrier and made in unfavourable weather conditions was magnificently carried out and reflects the greatest credit on all concerned.

"There can be little doubt that the hit they made was largely responsible for the *Bismarck* being finally brought to action and sunk."

---

[3] On the 26th, Lieutenant-Commander T. P. Goode led a force of Swordfish from *Ark Royal* which carried out the successful torpedo attack finally sealing the fate of *Bismarck*. The hit by Esmonde's squadron flooded the main boiler room and *Bismarck* lost 1000 tons of fuel oil

The man from Tipperary had been blooded. He would not have long to wait before once more he alone would sway the fortunes of war.[4]

---

[4] Eugene was not the only Esmonde intimately concerned with" the fate of *Bismarck*. In a convoy fewer than 20 miles from the Swordfish action was his twin brother, James, travelling home from the Gold Coast. The next day Captain Philip Vian, now Admiral of the Fleet, took his destroyers in to attack *Bismarck*. Second in this line of impudent little ships was *Zulu* and her engineer officer, Lieutenant-Commander Witham Esmonde.

CHAPTER 2: THE GERMAN DECISION

The French dockyard fitter in Brest became more infatuated with the farmer's daughter after the arrival of the battle cruisers, now joined by the *Prinz Eugen*. He noticed they were the centre of furious naval activity, heard that a transfer of local air forces was in operation and listened carefully to persistent rumours that the departure of the ships was imminent.

When his information reached London it was fitted into the general Intelligence mosaic consisting of reports from other agents and from air-reconnaissance patrols.

Consequently, in addition to the "Channel Stop" move, a series of conferences was held between Admiralty and Air Ministry planners which led on April 29th, 1941 — even before the *Bismarck* action — to an Air Ministry letter to the three Air Commands saying:

> There is reason to expect that the *Scharnhorst* and *Gneisenau* may attempt to reach a German port up the Channel route during the period April 30th to May 4th inclusive. It is considered probable that the Straits of Dover will be navigated in darkness.

To meet this threat, Coastal Command was ordered to establish dusk-to-dawn reconnaissances over and off Brest and up the Channel. Fighter Command organised down Channel sweeps against enemy coastal shipping generally, and Bomber Command were instructed to prepare striking forces should the reconnaissances show the enemy to have left Brest.

In the light of later events, the concluding paragraph of the letter was unfortunate:

> It is considered unlikely that the enemy would attempt the passage of the Straits in daylight. If, however, this should be attempted, *a unique opportunity will be offered to both our surface craft and air striking force to engage the enemy ships in force whilst in the Straits of Dover.*

Ten months before it happened the Admiralty and Air Ministry had warned their forces that a Channel dash was possible. Even the likelihood of a daylight crash through the Straits had been envisaged.

The plan to counter this enemy move was called "Operation Fuller", and on May 1st the Bomber Command part in it was laid down by the Commander-in-Chief, Air Marshal Sir Richard Peirse.

"If the passage of the ships is attempted," he said, "they will be attacked by surface craft and aircraft by day. It is not intended that aircraft should attack by night. The operation will be known by the codeword FULLER and the order putting it into effect will be EXECUTIVE FULLER."

At this stage it is clear that Bomber Command were prepared well in advance for daylight attacks. Indeed, the Admiralty and Air Ministry were thinking so far ahead that they had conceived a counter-plan for an operation not yet considered by the enemy.

It was the mortal blow to the *Bismarck* which convinced the German Navy of its need for revolutionary planning. Although the presence of the *Scharnhorst*, *Gneisenau* and *Prinz Eugen* in Brest was in itself a strategic advantage, it was an advantage which could not be exploited unless the port could be used freely as a front-line base for raiding operations in support of the U-boat offensive.

The Naval High Command was sufficiently astute to realise that the *Bismarck*'s action against *Hood* and *Prince of Wales* had been one of the more lucky incidents of the war. There was almost no likelihood, for instance, of *Tirpitz* being able to repeat the performance. They would have to regard the northern route round Iceland and through the Denmark Strait as effectively blocked and find some new way of sending ships into the Atlantic.

Not once in the history of the modern German Navy had theoretical planning foreseen use of the English Channel as a safe route for German ships. The Royal Navy's supremacy on the surface was acknowledged, even emphasised by occasional challenges, and the U-boat Arm had been created to close the power-gap between the two navies. Even so, to pass ships through the Channel would not be mere daring, it would be foolhardy.

Yet on May 30th the naval command in France sent a memorandum to the War Staff in Berlin containing the startling suggestion that the Channel was the natural alternative to the northern passage.

> The possibility of bringing heavy ships through the English Channel should be carefully examined, said the memorandum. The route is shorter than the Iceland passage; there are good escort possibilities, both air and sea; enemy radar could be jammed; superior enemy units would not be present; and the passage would be in the close proximity of our own harbours to which ships could be taken in the event of breakdowns.
>
> The obvious disadvantages include the difficulty of navigation in narrow waters; the undoubted fact that our ships would not pass unobserved by the enemy; and the danger

from mines, torpedo boats, torpedo-carrying aircraft and dive-bombers.

The plan was novel, and Admiral Raeder, C-in-C of the German Navy, although giving it little serious thought, was prepared to try a "dummy" east-west run with a cruiser. In an order to all commands, on May 31st, he said:

> The question of a possible passage through the English Channel must be carefully examined. Group commanders are requested to give their views and to submit draft operational orders for the passage through the Channel of one cruiser.
>
> Independent of the examination to be made by Group commanders the Naval War Staff at present cannot approve the use of the Channel as a breakout route.

Raeder's principal reason for objecting to the Channel route was that in the event of torpedo attack, the minesweepers could not sweep a wide enough path through minefields for the cruiser to take avoiding action. In conclusion he wrote:

> The Naval War Staff therefore consider an unobserved and safe escape through the Channel to be impossible.

At the end of May, then, the Royal Navy and RAF had a plan to meet a threat which in the reverse direction the enemy considered "impossible".

The enemy had not made the passage between April 30th and May 4th, as thought probable by the Air Ministry, but the view that a Channel dash was still likely prevailed and OPERATION FULLER remained in force.

On September 8th the Air Officer Commanding, Coastal Command, Air Chief Marshal Sir Philip Joubert, issued an Operational Instruction which said:

Prior warning of a passage through the Channel may not be received. The intention is to destroy the major enemy units on passage from Brest to a German port.

If practicable the torpedo attack from Thorney Island will be launched to synchronise with the bombing attack in order to take advantage of the fighter cover provided for the bombers.

Meanwhile, at the request of the Admiralty, Bomber Command mounted a night-bombing offensive on the Brest ships. If photographic reconnaissance produced evidence of severe damage, then the Admiralty could divert much-needed heavy units from Atlantic convoy coverage to theatres where their presence was becoming imperative.

Soon these nightly raids on Brest docks became a familiar part of the nation's daily life. In countless homes there were chuckles when the BBC's nine o'clock news announcer reported that a number of our bombers had visited Brest. To the layman it seemed inconceivable that Brest docks could be raided so many times and the ships not hit. Yet only one of these "Ugly Sisters", as the RAF called them, was seriously hit, while the other two escaped with minor damage.

At this time Hitler's celebrated intuition intervened in the Naval War Staff's calculations. He was convinced that Britain intended to invade Norway — a military adventure which would deprive Germany of Scandinavian iron ore and safeguard the passage of Russian convoys. It appeared to Hitler that these objectives alone would be worth while to an enemy who knew his business.

On September 17th Admiral Raeder attended a conference at which he was asked to report on his plans for employment of heavy ships in the Atlantic. Before he could properly begin, Hitler interrupted and suggested a different scheme.

"The Atlantic can be left to the U-boats," he announced decisively. "Your battleships, all your major units, must be stationed along the Norwegian coast. There they can be of some use" — he smiled at his own heavy sarcasm — "in guarding Norway against invasion. Anyway they will be safer from air attack there than in Brest, where three of them seem to be caught in a nice mess. What's going to happen to those?"

Patiently, the Commander-in-Chief explained in detail the rate of Allied losses at sea, the meaning of such losses to the war machine and his own plans for sending the big ships out to attack in the deep mid-Atlantic, where convoys thought they were safest.

For the moment Hitler was pacified. His obsession about an invasion of Norway, however, forced Raeder to consider sending the *Tirpitz* to Trondheim.

At another conference in November the subject was brought up again, and Hitler produced a map of the Norwegian coast on which were marked areas in which the *Scharnhorst, Gneisenau* and *Prinz Eugen* could operate defensively.

"But they are in Brest," protested Raeder.

"Get them back, then," retorted Hitler.

Another fierce argument ensued, and eventually Hitler calmed down sufficiently to cause Raeder to risk mentioning another possible Atlantic operation.

The pocket battleship *Admiral Scheer* had completed a refit and was ready for sea.

"I intend sending *Scheer* into the Atlantic. Now that it is winter she might be able to get through the Denmark Strait under cover of darkness. Have I your approval, *mein Führer?*"

"No," shouted the now enraged Hitler. "The Atlantic is not important, neither is the Indian Ocean, for that matter. There is only one important sea, and that is Norwegian coastal waters. The Norwegian Sea is vital. The *Scheer* must go to Trondheim or Narvik. Choose which is best."

After further discussion, Raeder was fortunate enough to hold his own on the question of the Brest ships.

In December the RAF bomber offensive against Brest increased, but for the first time there were indications in reconnaissance photographs that the ships were not only escaping serious damage but might be preparing for sea. Confirmation of this came in a continuous stream of intelligence from the "dockyard fitter".

On Christmas Eve the Admiralty ordered seven submarines to form an iron ring round the approaches to Brest. This meant that the submarine training squadrons at home and operational flotillas in the Mediterranean had to be weakened. It was an effort that could be sustained only temporarily.

Three days later Combined Operations launched the famous commando raid on Vaagso, an island off the Norwegian coast, and a diversionary raid on the Lofoten Islands. Designed to destroy industrial plants and defence points, these raids achieved an object of far greater, if less tangible, importance.

They convinced Hitler that his intuition was right again. The invasion of Norway was imminent. At another of his naval conferences on the 29th he demanded that the *Scharnhorst* and *Gneisenau* be returned to home waters to be fitted out for the defence of Norway. He referred to Raeder's plan to send a cruiser through the Channel to the Atlantic and insisted that the Channel route should be used for the west-east run.

Raeder replied:

"It is impossible to safeguard the route sufficiently. It is also impossible to evade air attacks in the narrow channels which might or might not be swept clear of mines."

His arguments had little effect upon Hitler.

"If the British go about things properly," declared the Führer, "they will attack northern Norway at several points. By means of an all-out attack with their fleet and landing troops they will try to displace us there, take Narvik if possible, and thus exert pressure on Sweden and Finland. This might be of decisive importance for the outcome of the war.

"The German fleet must therefore use all its forces for the defence of Norway. It would be expedient to transfer all battleships and pocket battleships there for this purpose.

"The return of the Brest ships is therefore most desirable."

He explained how this could be done. Rather than undertake any special working-up programme to train crews and test the efficiency of machinery and precision instruments, the ships should put out from Brest without any previous movement, so that they would take their opponents completely by surprise.

In view of the British intelligence services, "any preliminary exercise would lead to intensified torpedo and bomb attacks which sooner or later would damage the ships".

The vessels should sail in bad weather, when the RAF would be out of action, even if this meant increasing navigational difficulties for the German crews. As the main British fleet barred the Iceland passage, withdrawal could be made only through the Channel. Then came the chance for Hitler to express his spite against Raeder.

"If the Channel route is impossible," he almost shouted, "the Brest ships must be decommissioned and the guns dismantled and sent with the crews to Norway. In any case, battleships have no place in future wars and I doubt if they are much use now."

White-faced, Raeder stood silent. It was his Deputy Chief of Staff, Vice-Admiral Fricke, who dared to oppose the dictator's views. The best he could do was to extract permission to explore the position again.

The German Naval War Staff diary reads:

> This demand from the Highest Authority produced a new and essentially strategic factor for the War Staff; the withdrawal of the Battleship Group from the Atlantic area.
>
> By doing this the diversionary effect of Brest which compels the enemy to split up his Home Fleet to use heavy ships to protect his convoys in the Atlantic will cease to exist. The enemy ships tied up by our Brest force will now be released for operations in the Mediterranean or the Far East.

On January 2nd, 1942, the Royal Navy's submarine "iron ring" outside Brest could be maintained no longer. High submarine losses in the Mediterranean and a bottleneck in the training programme made the need for these submarines urgent. They were withdrawn and reliance for news of movements from Brest placed upon Coastal Command reconnaissances.

The next day Admiral Raeder received a report from his French headquarters saying:

> We must strongly advise against a withdrawal of the Brest ships through the Channel. A disappearance from the Atlantic will be regarded rightly by the enemy, by our allies and by the German people as a lost battle. Their presence in Brest is the right thing even if we have to reckon with heavy damage and lengthy repairs. Their employment in Norway will be no compensation for their withdrawal.
>
> If, as the Commander-in-Chief of the Luftwaffe has stated, the air protection of Brest cannot be maintained at its previous level, then the last measure remaining is the dismantling of the ships.

> If the Navy is confronted by the Supreme Commander of
> the Armed Forces with the question: break through or
> dismantle, then with heavy hearts we would prefer temporary
> dismantling to the break through with its enormous risks, as
> the former would be made good by returning the guns in the
> event of a change in the situation, whereas the loss of these
> valuable ships and their crews will produce *only* loss without
> *any* profit.

This report was followed by another from the naval
headquarters in Norway itself. Far from supporting the Führer,
it said:

> It is urged that there should be no withdrawal from Brest.
> There is the great risk that we shall lose one ship and suffer
> serious damage to a second at least. There are also strategic
> reasons entailing the tying down of heavy enemy units which
> might be more profitably used against us elsewhere.
> We must protest at any suggestion of dismantling their
> guns. This might have grave consequences in respect of
> morale throughout the Service.

Accepting the merits of both reports, Raeder proposed to
Hitler that the ships should stay in Brest, maintain strategic
advantages and should neither be laid up nor dismantled.

Hitler was chewing firmly on the Norwegian bit. Irritated by
the Naval High Command's persistent refusal to meet his
wishes, he summoned staffs of the three Services to his
"Wolf's Redoubt" to give them a lecture which amounted to
blunt orders none dare disobey.

Against the advice of the naval chiefs, and although the Air
Force could not guarantee complete protection with the 250
fighters available on the Channel coast, he decided to bring the

Brest ships home through the Channel. He demanded three prerequisites:

> 1. Movements of the three ships to be reduced to a minimum before the start of the operation.
> 2. The ships must leave Brest by night, so that when passing through the Channel they could use daylight for the most effective defence.
> 3. From early dawn to twilight the ships must have the maximum fighter cover possible.

From a man absorbed with land operations and whose acquaintanceship with ships was confined to an afternoon rowing on the Alster, these points were unexpectedly pertinent. Inside this framework the Naval Staff would fit the details, such as tides and weather, about which he was neither interested nor cared. His reasoning showed few weaknesses.

"The naval force at Brest has, above all, the welcome effect of tying up enemy forces and diverting them from making attacks on the German homeland. This advantage will last as long as the enemy considers himself compelled to attack because the ships are undamaged.

"If I could see any chance of the ships remaining undamaged for four or five months and thereafter be employed on operations in the Atlantic, I might feel more inclined to consider leaving them at Brest.

"Since such a development is not to be expected, I am determined to withdraw the ships from Brest to avoid exposing them to chance hits day after day. Moreover, the Russians are likely to join the English in attacking us through Norway, therefore the entire German fleet is required along the Norwegian coast for purposes of defence."

Vice-Admiral Ciliax, commander of the Brest battle squadron, agreed with Hitler that there were certain conditions on which the success of the operation might depend, and listed as his most important the element of surprise. Secrecy was to be the keynote of the planning. He confirmed that the Channel route offered the only hope, the northern route being out of the question because of the lack of training of the German crews, the lack of air support and the disposition of the British Home Fleet.

Then Hitler gave his *coup de grâce* to Raeder.

"The Brest group," he said, "are like a patient suffering from cancer who is doomed unless he submits to an operation. An operation, on the other hand, even though it might have to be drastic, affords some hope that the patient's life might be saved. The passage up Channel will be such an operation. Therefore the Channel operation has to be attempted.

"You can count on this; from my previous experience I do not believe the British capable of the conception and execution of lightning decisions such as will be required for the transfer of their air and sea forces to meet the boldness of our operation."

The decision was made. Far from dismantling the great ships, the Germans were to fight them through waters untrammelled in war by an enemy of England for three centuries. It would be seen if the decision was right.

Bomber Command, which had maintained the prolonged offensive against Brest to the extent that it forced Hitler's hand, began to ease the weight of the attack as losses mounted. The bombers being thrown in by day and night had to face the most dangerous and deadly anti-aircraft fire on the Continent.

In addition they had to press home their attacks against fighters and balloons in the worst possible weather. To do this not once, not twice, but time and time again called for a high degree of sustained courage.

Sergeant J. S. Boucher, a navigator of No144 Squadron flying Hampdens, gave this account of one raid made in daylight:

"We broke cloud over Ushant at 900 feet. None of us had much experience in flying in daylight, and having experienced the fierceness of the target at 12,000 feet at night, we felt a little apprehensive, to say the least — but we did not share our thoughts openly.

"We zigzagged in and out of cloud as we approached the coast. Everyone was strangely silent — apart from my curt navigational instructions — until the rear-gunner, who was experiencing his first operational flight, asked what the 'tapping noise' was. The wireless operator told him it was only light flak bursting as it hit the wings and fuselage.

"We broke cloud again long enough for me to give the pilot a course over the docks. The flak grew more intense and though flying in cloud the aircraft was repeatedly hit. We could see the criss-cross of red tracer shells through the cloud haze a few yards in front of us. It seemed that all the antiaircraft defences of the docks — as well as the battle cruisers — were directed at this one aircraft: and this was probably the case.

"The Hampden broke cloud again at 900 feet and I picked out the target a mile and a half ahead. To make a proper run up under such conditions would have been impossible if one was to survive to complete the task. I leaned over my bomb-sight and pressed the tit. For a few fleeting moments I could see the German gunners frantically firing at us. They seemed so close that I felt myself to be before a firing squad.

"The pilot opened the throttle and we roared into cloud again. A second later there was a yellow flash as a shell exploded, shattering the perspex nose of my cabin and driving me backwards under the floor of the pilot's cockpit. Stunned for a moment, I tried to open my eyes, but the pain was too great. I felt wet blood on my face.

"The gaping hole in the nose let the wind whistle through, blowing out my maps and log through the pilot's cockpit window. Now that we were in cloud again we were relatively safe and I was able to give the pilot a rough course home."

This crew rested only for a few days before returning again to Brest.

During the summer the Swordfish torpedo-bomber squadron commanded by Eugene Esmonde had been transferred to the *Ark Royal*, the aircraft carrier which had defied all attempts by enemy propaganda to sink her. As famous in Germany as in Britain, she was a prize eagerly sought and cherished by the German Navy and Luftwaffe; therefore it was only necessary to apply the law of averages to realise that at some time one of the innumerable attacks made on her would succeed.

It happened on November 13th. A torpedo struck the indomitable ship amidships and she listed over heavily on one side, writhing in agony. It was a mortal blow, and the destroyer escort closed to take off the crew.

Eugene Esmonde was about to slither down her side when he suddenly recalled that on board was his prized possession — a full-dress uniform with cocked hat, frock coat and sword. This would have been dismissed as a passing thought at a time when his ship was sinking and another torpedo might strike her at any moment, but for an unexpected twinge of conscious and sartorial pride.

He had not paid for it; therefore it was not his to lose. Also it was unworn. Turning back, he dodged through debris, crawled down passageways and finally reached his cabin, which by then was facing upwards to the sky.

Standing on the inner bulkhead, now the deck, he took the uniform from his leaning wardrobe and laid it carefully in front him. Then he stripped and proceeded to clothe himself meticulously. By laying his head to one side he was able to look at himself in the almost horizontal mirror and, at last satisfied, he gave his cocked hat a slightly rakish tug, pulled down the back of his frock-coat, hitched up the sword and crawled back to the dangerously slanting deck.

About forty-odd sailors crowded on a destroyer's foredeck saw him through the smoke and called out:

"Here, sir. This way."

Unhurriedly, Esmonde leaned back against the sloping side and made his way down like a crab. At the bottom he stood upright and leapt lightly across to the destroyer.

The oil-covered, spellbound sailors gazed with open-mouthed astonishment at this apparition; the younger reservists had probably never seen an officer in full-dress uniform. Centuries of rigid discipline came to their rescue and, despite the alarming urgency of the moment, those closest to Esmonde came shakily to attention and saluted.

Eugene replied with solemn formality, and in a fraction of time a strangely ceremonious ritual from an already bygone age was carried out against a background of a great ship in her death-throes with the hissing of escaping steam and the grinding of twisted girders providing the accompaniment.

In December the squadron re-formed at Lee-on-Solent, a depleted 825 Squadron with only six Swordfish, seven pilots, six observers and six air-gunners. Of these, only half were trained men, the remainder replacements.

Esmonde was fighting for personnel and aircraft to bring the squadron back to full strength when late in January the squadron commanders were ordered to a special briefing. With Esmonde were the commanders of other squadrons, including 829, then close to being at full strength.

Senior officers from the Admiralty and Flag Officer (Air) Staff were present at this conference, which was opened with the warning that all proceedings were to be regarded as secret.

The eagerly impatient fliers had not long to wait for the purpose. After describing the events leading up to recent information that the Brest ships might be preparing to break out, the briefing officer said:

"We believe that an enemy dash up Channel is imminent. We believe also that he will attempt to run through the Straits of Dover under cover of darkness about two hours before dawn, when tides and high water levels will be most favourable.

"There is only one way we can prevent this and destroy him — by throwing in the greatest available torpedo fire-power by combined air and sea attacks. It is intended therefore that Swordfish of the Fleet Air Arm and Coastal Command torpedo bombers should stand by to support light naval forces for this purpose.

"It will be pretty fierce when it starts. But with the protection of darkness and a lot of things happening all at the same time, the Swordfish should have a chance of delivering their attacks and getting away. We want the big chaps crippled so that heavier forces can sink them at will.

"It has been decided not to assign squadrons to this duty, but to call for one squadron commander to volunteer for himself as leader and on behalf of his squadron."

He concluded with the usual assurances that failure to volunteer would in no way interfere with an officer's record.

As he finished speaking there was a moment's silence while the implications of the request were absorbed by all present.

It was broken by a quiet, decisive voice from the middle of the room, and before he could finish, his words were being echoed by every commander present. But the small, bright-eyed figure of Eugene Esmonde had caught attention — the half-formed 825 Squadron had volunteered.

CHAPTER 3: THE SIMPLE BATTLE

Once the decision had been made to send the Brest ships home up the Channel, the German Navy and Luftwaffe devoted their resources to what one staff officer cynically described as "the burial of our ships at sea". In days not so long ago he would have been proven an accurate prophet.

At the dawn of 1942 he worried unduly: there was nothing in the British counter plan, "Fuller", to inspire fear. No adventurous spirit had come forward to throw down the glove to the enemy and dare him to invade our English Channel. There was no Drake or Nelson, Beatty or Jellicoe to compose a bold epitaph for the German Navy; no challenging assertion that the enemy would "founder on his own misjudgement".

The planning staffs either failed to recognise the deadly blow a successful Channel dash would deal to Britain's prestige everywhere, and not only then, but for generations to come, or they were content to assume that if David could do it once, he might be reasonably expected to do it again.

"Fuller" was destined to be abortive because the forces assigned to it were puny. It was based on the Admiralty concept of a "simple" battle wherein all forces would be thrown into the action without delay. Local commands would have freedom to operate according to the developing scene, and it was thought that too much detailed planning would restrict commanders at times when quick decision would prove imperative.

This meant that "Fuller" was in itself a contradiction, for the "simple battle" formula presupposes that the forces to be thrown into a massed attack are heavy enough to carry the day by sheer weight alone, if necessary. "Fuller's" forces would hardly be sufficient to guard the smallest South American republic.

Yet the Admiralty had consistently advocated the Channel passage as the logical route for the enemy ships. During January a stream of intelligence reports gave warning of hustle and bustle in Brest. Fighter and Coastal Commands supplied evidence of destroyer and E-boat flotillas passing through the Channel in the direction of Brest; of mine-sweeping activities along the French coast.

Events gathered momentum as the gap between plans and their execution narrowed daily.

On January 22nd three destroyers and six E-boats were shown by photographs to be anchored in the harbour, and on the 23rd Coastal Command photographic reconnaissance revealed the presence of *Tirpitz* at Trondheim.

The Admiralty interpreted the movement of *Tirpitz* as being intended to divert our attention from Brest, and in an appreciation the next day said:

> The *Scharnhorst* and *Prinz Eugen* can be expected to sail from Brest any time after today, January 24th. *Gneisenau* is not fully seaworthy and cannot sail until about the end of January. It is not considered that the ships are fully efficient yet.

On the 25th the German 5th Destroyer Flotilla moved south from the North Sea through the Channel. In the Dover approaches the destroyer *Bruno Heinemann* struck a mine and sank.

Later the same day Admiral Sir Max Horton, Flag Officer Commanding submarines, sent an "All Round" signal saying:

On the last day of January, at Lee-on-Solent, Esmonde was applying a rigorous training programme in torpedo attacks to both himself and his crews. No reinforcements had been sent and he thought with envy of the other squadrons also at Lee and their twenty-four serviceable Swordfish. He could hardly claim any of these, thereby earning the everlasting fury of his fellow commanders. In any case, it seemed inconceivable to him that the Admiralty would allow 825 to remain at half strength while the emergency for which he had volunteered still applied.

He confided as much to one of his most experienced observers, Sub-Lieutenant Edgar Lee, RNVR, a smooth-faced youngster barely turned twenty who had served in the squadron during the *Ark Royal* days. Of much the same build as his commander, but with fair hair and a lighter complexion, and sharing the same love of the air, Edgar Lee was devoted to Esmonde despite the strict discipline to which the squadron was subjected. Esmonde enjoyed an easy companionship with his officers outside duty hours. Otherwise he was almost feared for his harsh treatment of any unfortunate breach of what he regarded as necessary formalities.

This evening the squadron officers had gone to bed early, tired by the day's exercises and brooding bitterly on the programme for tomorrow. Suddenly messengers burst into the cabins, shook each occupant and passed the message:

"There's a flap on. Lieutenant-Commander Esmonde wants you in the briefing-room right away ready for flying."

Sub-Lieutenant Lee clambered out of bed, stuck his legs into flying-boots, his arms into a jacket and scampered across to the briefing-room. On the way he decided to make an urgent detour to the toilet. This made him late for the briefing.

Esmonde eyed him coldly and continued his address:

"We have just been told that the Brest ships might make a Channel dash tonight. The squadron is at fifteen minutes' notice, and I want all crews in their aircraft ready to take off. We will make a crescent attack in sub flights. That's all. Get cracking."

Throughout the night air and ground crews stayed at their aircraft for the expected word of an enemy sighting. But it was a false alarm, and at dawn they climbed, cramped and cold, from cockpits, all tension drained away and exhausted by the strain of waiting.

Esmonde shouted across to Lee:

"Here a minute."

"Yes, sir."

"What made you late for briefing? Everyone else was there when you arrived."

Lee shuffled uncomfortably.

"I'm sorry, sir. I thought there would be time to visit the heads."[5]

Esmonde's dark eyes hardened.

"When a flap is on, nothing is more important than getting to the briefing-room at once, do you understand? You, of all people, ought to know better. From now on you will be the first to arrive in any emergency briefing. That is an order which I don't think you should ever fail to carry out."

The anger died away and his eyes softened.

"Anyway, Lee, there will be plenty of opportunity for that sort of thing in the air once this particular balloon goes up."

---

[5] A naval term for toilet.

There were few things wrong with Esmonde's squadron — such was the nature of the commander.

A few days later the squadron was transferred to Manston in Kent to take part in the "Channel Stop" by flying patrols over the Dover Straits. At Manston they would be strategically placed to lead the attack on the Brest ships should they reach Dover.

Esmonde's first task was to train his crews in this new work. Two of his pilots and four of the observers had had no operational experience. Only his air-gunners were fully trained and operational and one, Leading Airman A. L. Johnson, had won the Distinguished Service Medal for his part in the *Bismarck* attack.

In the RAF mess at Manston, Esmonde told Wing Commander T. P. Gleave, the station commander: "I shall need a month to get my chaps used to this sort of thing. I'll have the night ops flown by alternate sub flights and the one not on night duty can train by day."

Gleave nodded his agreement. But the Swordfish of 825 Squadron were not to be allowed anything like a month. In little more than a week this gallant handful of eighteen men would face the war's greatest challenge.

At the beginning of February the Admiralty were convinced that the enemy ships were being exercised in the bay outside Brest. As a warning to all commands concerned, they issued a second appreciation which discussed the alternative routes the enemy might take in his race for home waters.

Dated February 2nd, the appreciation said:

> The Brest ships cannot be fully efficient yet; although they have led a charmed life the Germans must be anxious to get them away to a safer harbour. Only if we can anticipate the

plan of their departure can our chances of destroying them be good.

There are three, possibly five, large and five small destroyers at Brest, all of which have recently arrived. Mine-sweeping operations in the approaches to Brest have recently been seen. There has been no distinctive shape detected in any of the air reconnaissances flown by the Germans in the vicinity of Brest. These are indications of movement, but no indication of its direction.

The short cut for the German ships is via the English Channel. It is 240 miles from Brest to Cherbourg and another 120 miles from Cherbourg to the Dover Straits. Whilst ships could make the passage from Brest to Cherbourg, or from Cherbourg to the Dover Straits, in the same dark period, they could not make the complete passage from Brest to the Dover Straits in one dark period.

At first sight this passage up the Channel seems hazardous for the Germans. It is probable, however, that, as their heavy ships are not fully efficient, they would prefer such a passage relying for their security on the destroyers and aircraft which are efficient and knowing full well that we have no heavy ships with which to oppose them in the Channel.

We might well therefore find the two battle cruisers and the heavy 3" cruiser with five large and five small destroyers, also, say, 20 fighters constantly overhead (with reinforcements within call) proceeding up the Channel.

To meet this sortie we have about six MTBs at Dover, but no destroyers with torpedo armament.

Our bombers have shown that we cannot place much reliance on them to damage the enemy, whilst our Coastal Command torpedo-bomber aircraft will not muster more than nine.

Taking all factors into consideration, it appears that the German ships can pass East up the Channel with much less risk than they will incur if they attempt an ocean passage.

It would seem from this appreciation that the Admiralty were not only prepared for an enemy attempt at a Channel dash but accepted the probability that it might succeed. Apart from the Dover motor-torpedo boats and the transfer of Eugene Esmonde's Swordfish to Manston, the Navy had made no move to block the Channel against enemy heavy ships.

The only precaution taken now was to send the submarine *Sealion* on patrol off the Brest approaches.

During the evening naval liaison officers to the three Air Commands were summoned to the Admiralty for a lecture based on the second appreciation. During this conference an officer who must be nameless, because he is no longer junior, asked:

"Would it not be possible for the Home Fleet or part of it to be stationed somewhere down the east coast, from where they could sail to intercept the enemy off the Dutch coast if the Straits were penetrated?"

This logical, but naive, question received the reply:

"The First Sea Lord has stated plainly that on no account will he bring heavy ships south, where they will be exposed to enemy air attack, torpedo-boat attack and risk being damaged on our own and enemy minefields."

The officer persisted:

"But surely the light forces already available will be totally inadequate to deal with an enemy battle fleet?"

"We have scraped together all that is at present available," was the curt answer.

Our "dockyard fitter" in Brest was particularly active at this time maintaining a constant stream of information which led later that night to Admiral Sir Max Horton, Flag Officer Commanding Submarines, sending a top-secret signal to all submarines in home waters saying:

The Admiralty signalled all naval and air commands concerned:

Admiralty now appreciate most probable course of action of enemy ships at Brest will be to break eastwards up the Channel and so to home waters.

The submarine *Sealion*, commanded by Lieutenant-Commander G. R. Colvin, RN, was sailing from Portsmouth that afternoon. At a briefing conference he was told:

"Your operational area is designed to intercept the enemy main units should they break out into the Atlantic or proceed south-eastwards to another Biscayan port."

As a further precaution, "Force H", the task force based at Gibraltar, was held at immediate notice, while Bomber Command intensified minelaying operations off the Friesian Isles.

There could be no further delay in alerting our air and sea forces. On February 4th the Admiralty and Air Ministry issued the signal: EXECUTIVE FULLER, which brought both Services to a state of immediate readiness for action.

Rear-Admiral Power, Assistant Chief of Naval Staff (Home Operations), who maintained liaison between the naval and air planners, held a series of personal talks with Air Chief Marshal Sir Philip Joubert, of Coastal Command, which concluded with the two officers deciding that not only would the enemy come up the Channel, but that he would do it soon and maintain a timetable which would bring him into the Dover Straits during darkness.

On the 5th Admiral Power drove hurriedly to Dover to pass Sir Philip's views on to Admiral Ramsay. His official report also mentions that he stayed the night to "obtain first-hand knowledge of the operations room at Dover and the possibilities of controlling traffic in the Channel with radar assistance".

Also discussed was the problem of bringing more torpedo power into the Dover defences. Admiral Ramsay shared the view that the enemy would reach the Straits in darkness, probably about two hours before dawn.

In London the following day Admiral Power reported on his talks with Sir Philip and Admiral Ramsay and, as a result, six destroyers at Harwich — veterans of the First War — were ordered to stand by for a possible attack under "Fuller"; the six Swordfish operating night patrols over the Straits were also brought into the "Fuller" orbit; and six more MTBs were stationed at Ramsgate to follow the Dover flotilla's attack. These forces were placed under the operational orders of Admiral Ramsay.

The signal to Esmonde's squadron said: *The Squadron Commander to operate only those crews which he considers would contribute to achievement of object.* With barely sufficient men to fly his planes, and with some of these not yet fully trained and operationally "green", there would be little choice.

It was impossible for these slender forces to be kept at immediate notice for an indefinite period. Nor could air reconnaissance be relied upon at night, although under favourable weather conditions sufficient warning could be given by day.

Meanwhile an important troop convoy for the Middle East was forming up in the Clyde in readiness to sail on February 16th. The Prime Minister sent a memorandum to the First Sea Lord:

This convoy is of vital importance to our land operations in the Middle East. It must get through with as little loss as possible. What is happening about the Brest ships?

Sir Dudley Pound was also aware of the danger to the convoy when it passed down into the Bay of Biscay. If the enemy was in any way informed of the equipment and troops carried in WS16 — code-name for the convoy — the Brest ships would almost certainly sail out to attack. It would be a battlefield of their own choosing, easily saturated by the Luftwaffe, and the surface attack could be adequately supported by U-boats from their Biscayan bases.

The first Sea Lord realised he would have to cover the convoy with a battle squadron; in a signal to the Commander-in-Chief, Home Fleet, he said:

Possibilities of Brest ships coming out appreciated but sailing of WS16 cannot be deferred. Request you sail Rodney[6] *to arrive Clyde am on Friday 15.*

In another signal to Gibraltar addressed to "Force H", he said:

As German battle cruisers may be tempted to operate in Atlantic, Force H is to proceed to Clyde to arrive not later than February 15. Object is to give protection to WS16, which will sail under the command of Admiral Sir James Somerville in Formidable.

The grand positioning of forces was beginning.

By this time persistent reports by his reconnaissance crews of large-scale minesweeping operations by the enemy along the Channel convinced Sir Philip Joubert that the time was

---

[6] *Rodney* needed refitting so badly that *Renown* was sent instead.

approaching to sound a note of urgent warning. In a Coastal Command appreciation on February 8th, which was remarkable for its accuracy, he said:

> There are four large destroyers and a number of small motor torpedo boats and minesweepers in Brest. There are indications that the number of destroyers may be increased. During the past few days all three big ships have been carrying out exercises in open waters and they should be reasonably ready for sea.
>
> As from the 10th the weather conditions in the Channel would be reasonably favourable for an attempted break through in darkness. On February 15th there will be no moon and the tidal conditions at Dover would favour a passage between 0400 and 0600 hours.
>
> Finally, the large number of destroyers and small torpedo boats that have been concentrated at Brest would seem to indicate an attempt to force a way up the Channel... any time after Tuesday, February 10th.

This appreciation had been approved in draft form by Admiral Power. That it was so correct could not be known at the time, and Sir Philip hesitated to act upon his own document. His available torpedo bomber forces were dispersed — No42 Squadron, consisting of fourteen Beauforts, was stationed at Leuchars, in Scotland, from where it could fly against the *Tirpitz*; No86 Squadron, of twelve aircraft reinforced by three Beauforts of No217 Squadron, were at St Eval in Cornwall to meet a breakout from Brest into the Atlantic; and the seven remaining aircraft of 217 Squadron were at Thorney Island, near Portsmouth.

The logical move for Sir Philip immediately he felt confident of his own predictions was to bring the Leuchars squadron south to meet the more urgent threat. This would have enabled his forces to attack together.

When he did so eventually, administrative difficulties led to a delay — a delay that was to bear heavily on the outcome of the battle. Although he could not be aware of it, Coastal Command was to be the victim of human error again at an even more vital moment. His staff officers, impressed with the secrecy surrounding "Fuller" and the stamp "Top Secret" on all documents, locked the plans carefully away in a safe and considered their contents too secret to be told to the air crews. Pilots had heard a "buzz", but few knew they might one day fly against an enemy battle fleet.

On Coastal Command rested responsibility for early sighting of the enemy, so three dusk-to-dawn patrols were established, which crossed over in areas extending from Brest to Boulogne. The first of these was called "Stopper", and covered the stretch from Brest to Ushant; the second, known as "Line SE.", covered from Ushant to the north-east corner of Brittany; the third, code-named "Habo", extended from Havre to Boulogne.

These patrols were designed to operate so that if one failed to sight the enemy there would be a good chance that the others would. Their times of take-off were related to the prevailing view that the ships would leave Brest to reach the Dover Straits in darkness, just before dawn; the aircraft were equipped with radar, which would provide the one hope of finding the enemy on dark nights and in bad weather.

Bomber Command were concerned only if confronted with an opportunity to attack in daylight. When "Fuller" had been brought into operation on the 4th, the Command had more than 300 bombers available for the operation. There was no provision in the plan for the degree of readiness at which they should be held, the Air Ministry deciding that this was a decision best left to the Air Officer Commanding, Sir Richard Peirse. After the 6th only 100 bombers were available to "Fuller".

Fighter Command's responsibilities were shouldered by No11 Group, embracing the Kenley, Hornchurch, Debden, Biggin Hill and Tangmere Wings. They were to escort the torpedo bombers and bombers while at the same time engaging the Luftwaffe umbrella under which the enemy was expected to sail.

By February 10th the situation in the Admiralty, Mediterranean and Home Commands was that the probability of an approaching Channel dash by the enemy was fully realised and the naval forces disposed as follows: the Home Fleet was split, with large units patrolling the Denmark Straits and the remainder sitting in Scapa Flow watching the operationally efficient *Tirpitz* at Trondheim; "Force H" was at sea, heading for the Clyde; the minelayers *Welshman* and *Manxman* had laid 1000 magnetic and contact mines between Ushant and Boulogne; the submarine *Sealion* was patrolling off Brest; and to block the Dover Straits were six Swordfish at Manston, the two MTB flotillas at Dover and Ramsgate and the six Harwich destroyers.

Facing this pathetically tiny force from the protection of Brest was the full armoured might of a battle squadron brooding under the wings of a Luftwaffe fighter force capable of providing greater air cover than any fleet had enjoyed before.

Admiral Ramsay's intention was to launch combined torpedo attacks by the MTBs and Swordfish in the hope of damaging the enemy while he was in range of the Dover guns. This was to be followed with an attack by the Harwich destroyers off the Belgian coast, where there would be freedom of movement unhampered by our minefields.

These naval operations were to be accompanied by heavy air attacks by Bomber and Coastal Commands adequately covered by fighters. If, as expected, the passage of the Germans took place at night during a moonlight period the Swordfish were to attack as a squadron; if the call to action came during a dark period they were to attack singly. Arrangements were made to have them directed by the RAF controller at Swingate.

Hurricane fighter-bombers were to drop flares over the enemy targets.

Appropriate orders were issued to each force, and the instruction: *Proceed in execution of previous orders* was all that was necessary to put "Fuller" into operation.

This was the "simple battle" envisaged by Admiral Power and his staff — in other words, it was intended to throw in all available forces at the earliest moment. The "simple battle" was a planner's phrase destined to have little meaning for the men who were to fight and die over and beyond that traditional British battlefield — the Straits of Dover.

CHAPTER 4: BREAKOUT

In contrast to the British counter-move loosely explained by an interchange of instructions between two Service Dements, the Germans had a clearly detailed plan called "Operation Cerberus" — although six decoy code-names were applied at various times to confuse British agents. It covered 120 foolscap pages of single-spaced typing and left individual commanders and responsible officers in no doubt of their duties in any emergency. It demanded strict adherence to each detail, stupid errors being impossible unless the officer was illiterate.

The hinge on which the Admiral Commanding Battleships, Vice-Admiral Ciliax,[7] hoped to force the Channel door at Dover was the essential element of surprise. Complete security, then, was the first requirement during the planning stage. His chief of Staff, Captain H. J. Reinicke, has told the United States Naval Institute:

"The most difficult thing for us in those days was to find a story for all who had something to do with the operation without knowing why. All these stories and a few deliberately inspired rumours had to be fitted into a big mosaic which might resemble the true picture without betraying it.

"Only Admiral Ciliax, the captains of the three big ships — Hoffmann of *Scharnhorst*, Fein of *Gneisenau* and Brinkmann of *Prinz Eugen* — myself and the senior destroyer officer shared with a few staff officers full knowledge of the real plan."

---

[7] Ciliax lives now in West Germany.

Under this dominant canopy of secrecy the principal problems facing the "Cerberus" planners were choice of route, date and time of departure and the most favourable time to reach the critical passage through the Dover Straits. Unfortunately their logic was too sound, their reasoning too faultless, their findings a model of intelligent planning.

Outside the security barriers the ships began to shake down for whatever task lay ahead. For long months they had been exposed to the frequent RAF attacks, which were not without some reward. A Coastal Command torpedo bomber which accompanied one raid had successfully hit the *Gneisenau*, causing damage which put her into dry dock for most of her enforced stay in Brest.

By the end of January, however, most of the damage to all three ships had been repaired. The necessary speed trials which followed were limited by the German fear of mines and submarines outside the harbour. In addition, the nine months under air attack, the camouflage, the carrying out of repairs in the permanent presence of large numbers of dockyard personnel, did not permit the exercising of weapons nor the cumbersome apparatus of clearing ships for emergency action.

When they did venture outside the harbour for brief practice runs, bad weather prevented orthodox gunnery exercises. The ships could be put to sea, but their standard of fighting efficiency was woefully low.

On January 30th Vice-Admiral Ciliax sent the following signal to Berlin:

Gneisenau has completed her first practice run. Weather rainy and visibility bad so that pre-arranged firing practice unable to be carried out. Engines completely ready.

Three days later *Scharnhorst* sailed in better weather and was able to spend the day in Iroise Bay, in which Brest is almost enclosed, steaming at 29 knots and carrying out full practice shoots with all calibres. On February 4th *Prinz Eugen* successfully completed her trials.

On her return to harbour that evening Ciliax informed Raeder that the Brest ships were ready for action.

The choice of route up Channel depended on three major conditions — a route which passed over deep water as far as possible and on which the danger of contact mines could be suitably reduced; a route which lay outside the range of British radar as far as possible; and a route favourable for high speeds and navigationally simple.

These conditions were embraced by the eventual choice, which lay roughly up the middle of the Channel as far as Boulogne, before running to within two miles of the French coast as it approached the Narrow Sea. Along such a route the enemy could make use of deep water which propellers could grip and give the full thrust necessary for high-speed steaming; it reduced the danger from moored and magnetic mines.

Radar stations along the English south coast were thought to have an effective range of not more than 35 miles, and the route took the ships outside this range until they would be almost in sight of the English coast anyway.

In the choice of a departure date, the German plan "Cerberus" said:

> The most favourable conditions for the undertaking are present at the time of the new moon; the dark nights provide protection against premature sighting of the formation and render more difficult the employment of enemy air and light forces; the great tidal effect of the spring tides reduce the

danger of mines in shallow water and the strong tidal stream will increase the speed of the formation by 4-5 knots.

The first new moon period, then, after the readiness of the ships had been reported was on February 15th. Accordingly "Cerberus" was planned to take place on the evening of X-day, February 11th.

Breakout time was related solely to the main danger point to the Germans, the Dover Straits, where the Royal Navy and RAF could be expected to stage a massed attack. At this point also the route necessarily ran into shallow water near the French coast and the danger from mines would increase.

"At first glance," said Operation Cerberus, "it appears tempting to pass *this point in the darkness of night.* This, however, will have the disadvantage that the ships will have to leave Brest in the forenoon and steam through the Channel in broad daylight. The enemy would receive warning from air reconnaissance in good time and will not only get ready his torpedo and bomber aircraft and MTB flotillas in the Straits, but might also bring his large units from Scapa Flow, which is only 450 miles from Terschelling, whereas the distance from Brest to Terschelling is 575 miles."

Admiral Ciliax assessed the dangers to his squadron as mines, the use of light naval forces and MTBs, the use of torpedo and bomber aircraft and lastly that of large units. Except for the mine danger, he said, all the British counter-measures had this in common — "that the later our intention to force a passage through the Channel becomes known and the more our defences are put into use, the less effective will they be. Therefore, if the stretch within and on both sides of the Dover Straits is regarded as the most dangerous because of it being covered by radar and our presence at night certain to become known, the answer must be that this section of the route must be covered in daylight, when we can best defend ourselves."

In support of this logical argument were the undoubted facts that in daylight he could meet torpedo and bomber attacks with effective anti-aircraft fire and fighter cover; surprise attack, such as radar spotting might cause at night, would not be possible; and the strength of the Luftwaffe cover would make it possible to bridge the daylight hours.

Passage through the Dover Straits at night would mean attacks from unseen torpedo boats and possibly destroyers. These forces could be met effectively only in daylight with the battle squadron's far superior fire-power and greater numerical superiority.

Having listed the advantages of a daylight passage through the Straits, the arguments against a night passage became frighteningly plausible. It seems inconceivable that the best and most experienced brains in the Royal Navy and Air Ministry failed to consider them — or, if they did, gave them scant attention.

The battle squadron would have no fighter cover and antiaircraft defences would be neutralised; the use of superior fire-power against MTBs and destroyers would be seriously impaired and, above all — this is important when related to our own appreciations — the daylight passage in the western Channel would surely lead to early discovery.

There was an undeniable case for passing up Channel during the dark and fighting a path through the Dover Straits in daylight. Zero hour for departure was to be 7.30 pm on the 11th, with arrival at the critical Straits timed for 11.30 am the next morning.

Suitable ports along the Channel, such as Cherbourg, Le Havre, Flushing and the Hook of Holland, were ordered to stand by as emergency harbours. Arrangements were made for the entire route to be swept by minesweepers, and marker boats were to be placed in pairs at intervals along its length — seven pairs marked the Channel route and nine the passage from Dover to home waters. Complete immunity against mines could not be guaranteed, so it was decided to reinforce the minesweeping flotillas based on the Channel ports and "blitz" the route through minefields between January 20th and February 10th.

An elaborate air defence plan was worked out under the code-name "Thunderbolt", with the youthful Fighter General Adolf Galland in command. The lessons of Norway and Crete, where air power harried naval forces mercilessly, and the recent sinking of the *Repulse* and *Prince of Wales* in analogous circumstances — these battleships were destroyed by Japanese torpedo bombers operating 400 miles from the nearest airfields — had not been lost on the Germans. Throughout the Channel passage their ships would be in easy striking distance of British torpedo bombers, and the Japanese victory of December 10th was not considered a happy augury for them.

Main source for the air umbrella designed to cover the battle squadron was the force of 250 fighters maintained along the Channel coast. As this number could not be flown all at the same time it was arranged that a force of sixteen fighters should be constantly overhead throughout the daylight hours, each sortie lasting for thirty-five minutes. Each wave would arrive ten minutes before the other left, so that for periods of twenty minutes of each hour there would be thirty-two fighters overhead. This would mean utilising the entire force throughout the day in alternating waves while leaving a large enough force on the ground to take off in strength to meet the British air attacks.

Galland placed aboard each of the big ships a fighter liaison officer equipped with a short-wave radio set for inter-ship communication. The senior of these, a Colonel Ibel, aboard *Scharnhorst)* was to give on-the-spot directions to the fighters above as attacks developed. Galland himself established headquarters at Le Touquet with subsidiary headquarters at Caen and Schipol in Holland, both of which were in contact with their local airfields and also with Galland at Le Touquet.

The setting up of such a complicated communications network required a series of "dummy" runs, and during the first days of February the Luftwaffe flew no fewer than 450 special sorties under which actual Channel dash conditions were simulated without causing the slightest alarm to our side. Ironically accurate was the code-name for these rehearsals — "The Beginning of Spring".

As in the naval plan, "Thunderbolt" depended largely on security for its success. Any noticeable transfer of large fighter forces would focus the RAF's attention in an embarrassing direction. The plan held down therefore that "only the circle of people who must without question have knowledge of it in order to carry out their work are to be initiated into the real aim of the undertaking.

"The Chief of the General Staff of the Third Luftwaffe Air Fleet will give consent for initiation and this has to be signed for on a written list with legible signatures.

"Secrecy will cease on X-day when it is certain that the enemy have sighted our ships."

Meanwhile the Luftwaffe's Director of Communications, General Martini, had recently completed successful experiments with a new and strictly secret method of jamming British radar stations along the south coast. From the beginning of February onwards he directed a planned operation of interference. Each day at dawn our radar stations were subjected to a few minutes of jamming which resembled atmospheric interference. The length of the jamming increased daily, until by February 11th our radar operators were thoroughly accustomed to the particular type of interference which they reported normally as caused by atmospheric conditions.

This cleverly executed plan was to be largely responsible for the delays in the British attack.

The weather had not carried decisive weight in Admiral Ciliax's plans, but forecasts for the 12th were encouraging. Meteorological reports indicated that the Channel would be fine in the morning with a stiff breeze. After midday the wind would drop and the weather would generally deteriorate for about three hours before clearing again. This would mean probable low cloud and visibility about the time the squadron reached the approaches to Dover.

The Luftwaffe's bomber forces were not overlooked. One wing was detached to the Channel coast to be called upon to bomb British sea forces should they attack in strength.

The German naval forces were organised to acquire a "snowball" effect as they moved up Channel. On the first leg the force would consist of *Scharnhorst*, *Gneisenau*, *Prinz Eugen* and six large destroyers. Once round the Cherbourg corner, this squadron would be joined by two E-boat flotillas numbering ten boats. Off Cap Gris Nez the squadron would take on the proportions of a main fleet when twenty-four more E-boats joined company, with gunboats, E-boats and minesweepers of the Western and Northern naval commands, bringing the total up to sixty-three ships.

At this point in the run the fighter umbrella would increase to its maximum and the bomber force would take off to lie in wait in the clouds for a suitable British target. This would be a formidable force; the six German destroyers were large modern ships compared with our small Harwich oldsters. The German E-boat was a larger, faster and more manoeuvrable boat than our MTB and the enemy had three to our one; he could call on a fighter force of 250 planes to engage our torpedo bombers and bombers.

The odds were mounting against us. It seems deplorable that Britain, the world's leading sea-power at the time, could not sustain an effort to field as strong a team as the enemy, who acknowledged our superiority, yet dared to challenge it.

On February 4th Admiral Ciliax raised his flag in *Scharnhorst* and issued his Operational Orders for the dash. They were prefaced with instructions that commanding officers of the escort forces should not be given copies until they had received the code-word "Ganges" — cover name for a decoy trip to the Pacific. On completion of the operation these orders were to be destroyed. They read:

> 1. The task is the execution of this eastward passage by the fullest use of the maximum speed of the formation. The task will be carried out at the time of the new moon. It is to be carried out if only one battle cruiser is ready on the day when the codeword is issued. It is cancelled if only *Prinz Eugen* is ready.
> 2. It is a bold and unheard of operation for the German Navy. It will succeed if these orders are strictly obeyed. There is no margin for interpretation. They must be adhered to at all times.
> 3. In the execution of the task I expect air attacks, attacks by light forces and the danger of mines. I regard the probability of attack by heavy enemy forces as remote, although it would be possible from his north Scottish bases if the enemy recognised our intentions at a very early stage and was

prepared to accept considerable risk. Artillery bombardment from shore is likely during the passage of the Dover Straits.

4. Ships will slip in following order — *Scharnhorst*, *Gneisenau* and *Prinz Eugen*, with escort forces taking station outside harbour in accordance with their instructions.

5. Do not seek combat, but only engage the enemy if the operation cannot otherwise be carried out. The task of proceeding eastwards quickly is paramount.

Something had to be done in Brest to kill rumours, some of which were becoming dangerously near the truth. Captain Reinicke telephoned a friend on the Admiral's staff in Paris, and that afternoon a signal went round the squadron inviting all commanding officers then in harbour to dine at the Paris headquarters of the Admiral Commanding, Western Group, at 8 pm on the 11th.

It was the sort of invitation no commander dared ignore or refuse unless he had good reason. About thirty signals were sent back to Paris accepting the invitation, and to any British agent it would seem unlikely that the ships could possibly leave harbour before the 14th — a day to get to Paris, a day there and a day back.

At the same time the Army Commander threw a cordon of troops round the port, barricaded every street and allowed only approved Frenchmen exit or entry. The city was sealed; the ships were ready; Galland's fighters were ready; General Martini and his technical team were patiently jamming the British radar stations in bursts of a few seconds, sometimes minutes.

On the evening of X-day, February 11th, 1942, the overture to the operation began. The roaring noise of boiler-room fans beat from the ships as steam pressure was raised; tugs with their red, white and green navigation lights moved across the still harbour-water taking their stations near the berths where the big ships lay; telephone, steam, water and other ship-to-shore lines were disconnected; shouted orders drifted across the docks with the dull murmur of three big ships coming awake after spending nine months in idleness. The anxious, shrill screams of destroyer and E-boat hooters occasionally punctured the activity as they hurried to their stations for leaving harbour. A fleet was taking shape — the first German force to challenge British supremacy in the Channel.

Senior commanders met aboard *Scharnhorst* for a last-minute conference with Admiral Ciliax. If there were agents in Brest who might be frantically trying to find out why there had been no officers leaving for their dinner appointment in Paris, they had little more than an hour in which to do it.

At 7 pm the Admiral wished his commanders good luck and they returned to their ships. In half an hour the signal to sail would blink from *Scharnhorst*'s bridge.

Then Bomber Command intervened. At precisely 7.30 pm the sirens wailed and all movement ceased in the harbour as the drone of the raiding force grew louder. Within a few minutes anti-aircraft guns were barking and a dense artificial fog was building up across the docks. Orders postponing the fleet's departure flashed from ship to ship, and more than 4000 German sailors, of whom only a handful knew their destination, settled down to wait for the "All Clear".

In the next two hours bombs fell on the docks well clear of the ships. In the occasional breaks in the artificial fog, dozens of flashlight bombs exploded overhead as photographic reconnaissance planes accompanying the bomber force took pictures which would show the heavy ships out of dock but safely tucked up in their berths. The expert photographic analysts in London would see from these pictures that while the enemy ships had left the repair yards, there was no evidence of abnormal activity in Brest.

Then it was quiet overhead; the last raider had retired. The "All Clear" sounded over the town and signals flashed again across the harbour. The huge, sleek *Scharnhorst* drifted slowly away from her berth, telegraphs clanged and her propellers churned the water.

The breakout from Brest had begun. The time — 9.45 pm.

Outside the boom defences of Brest, *Sealion* lay in wait; inside the town a British agent strove frantically to reach his radio set. The most vital element of all now for Britain was time — time to mass her forces and attack the enemy as he entered the Channel.

CHAPTER 5: THE DARK PASSAGE

Air Reconnaissance shows that on any day or night exercise there is a fifty per cent chance of enemy main units exercising in Iroise. If visibility sufficient and enemy patrols permit you may at your discretion close the area and attack. There is no information regarding enemy minefields or harbour defences in the area.

This signal from Sir Max Horton reached *Sealion* on February 7th as she lay off Brest. Her commanding officer, Lieutenant-Commander Colvin, was more worried about his own crew than the enemy. Consisting mostly of reservists, anyway, the ship's company had received twelve replacements on the morning of sailing, including the key man, the Torpedo Gunner's Mate. The First Lieutenant, Lieutenant E. P. Young, RNVR, had also joined just before sailing with two other new officers.

Colvin had no doubts about their courage — but they needed time to settle in and learn the whereabouts of every dial, lever and button, so that in emergencies there would be no fumbling.

Now he nosed *Sealion* towards Iroise Bay, hoping to sneak into the exercising area, fire his torpedoes and make good a withdrawal seawards. He was fully aware, and if his crew held similar views they gave no sign of it, that once the attack was made escape would be a bleak possibility; *Sealion* would almost certainly be destroyed. There were natural dangers to add spice to the adventure. The Iroise abounds with rocks and reefs largely uncharted, strong currents and treacherous tides.

Sealion saw nothing that day, or the next; but on the 9th she moved into the northern curve of the bay, in which stretched the lines of boom defences guarding Brest itself. It was shortly after midday, the weather was fine and the sea choppy. Through the periscope Colvin sighted the Whistle Buoy marking the end of the swept Channel into Brest. He would lie beneath it until darkness and then surface.

Later in the afternoon he received another signal from Sir Max's headquarters in London's Swiss Cottage saying:

> *As for as is known the enemy main units at Brest have not exercised during the last four days. There is nothing to indicate that any may have been hit by bombs and any one or all three ships may exercise at any time or even break port, though this latter course seems unlikely until further exercises have been carried out.*
>
> *I do not want you to go in unless all circumstances are in your opinion favourable.*

Colvin grimaced wryly — he was already in.

Nothing was sighted during daylight, and another signal from Sir Max said the enemy ships were still lying at their berths inside the harbour. At 8 pm Colvin brought *Sealion* to the surface and waited near the Whistle Buoy in case the enemy came out for night exercises.

In the next hour furious patrol-boat activity forced him to withdraw slightly, but he was still in good sight of the buoy. About five miles away patrol-boats fired coloured Very light recognition signals to a circling aircraft.

A little after 9 pm a Dornier bomber roared out of the darkness with cabin lights glowing and navigation lights on, swooped down to a height of not more than 200 feet and switched on searchlights. The beams swung ahead of *Sealion* as Colvin and the conning-tower crew tumbled down the hatchway of the already diving submarine.

Colvin stubbornly refused to retreat. He remained under water near the buoy for another hour, when suddenly the hydroplane operator reported the sound of approaching propellers. A few minutes later depth-charges tumbled down and the dreaded *tonk, tonk* of the explosions rattled through the submarine. Now was the time to get away.

The Whistle-Buoy-Wait, as one wag in the crew had dubbed the operation, was repeated on the next day without result and a further patient and probably lengthy wait was planned for the 11th.

In his subsequent Report of Proceedings, Lieutenant-Commander Colvin wrote:

> I arranged my arrival at the Whistle Buoy on Wednesday, February 11th, to coincide with the turning of the tide and with favourable tides the submarine entered the exercising area again at 1200. The weather was fine, visibility good and sea becoming a little rough.
>
> It was a perfect day for reconnaissance. Had any ships been in the Iroise I must have seen them.
>
> By 1340, no big ships having been seen and the tide now running south, I set course to withdraw along the same route, as my batteries needed topping up in case of emergency.

Colvin brought *Sealion* back to the Whistle Buoy at dusk and waited. At 7.30 pm — departure hour for the enemy fleet — he was in position to fire his torpedoes at the big ships should they pass out of Brest. From the conning-tower he heard the drone of engines and the faint crack of guns. The brilliant flashes of bursting bombs slapped against the still, black night. Bomber Command had arrived, unwittingly ruining any chance *Sealion* might have had.

At 8.25 pm — an hour after the enemy should have steamed into his sights and before the breakout began — *Sealion* could wait no longer. She dived and withdrew to charge her batteries before returning the next day for another vain Whistle-Buoy-Wait.

Britain's first line of defence had been breached.

Inside Brest the "dockyard fitter" was cycling furiously up and down the streets in an attempt to find a weak link in the security cordon round the city. He had heard rumours, he had seen the preparations in the docks and the trained eye of a naval officer was not deceived. The ships were not sailing for an exercise. More likely in his view they were sailing operationally.

For days he had watched and waited. After darkness on the 11th he had recognised the sound of ships raising steam, and set off on his bicycle to visit the farmer's daughter at the farm five miles away.

Approaching the city limits, he had seen in the distance the barriers erected across the street by the German Army. Confident of his safety, he approached the roadblock, dismounted and called out indignantly to the nearest guard to let him through. The German shook his head and a sergeant came round from the other side. The argument seemed everlasting, and as the precious minutes passed, the fitter became fretful. Then he gave up in disgust, mounted his cycle and pedalled off down a side street.

He attempted to argue his way through one barricade after another until well after midnight. Then he returned to his lodgings, vaguely hoping the enemy had decided on a course that would enable his news, when it did reach England, to be of some use.

A second line of defence against an unobserved breakout had failed, and the enemy, already round the Breton tip, had entered the English Channel.

The echoes of midnight chimes had barely died away when Brest awakened to the sound of screaming sirens. The second of the almost nightly bomber raids had begun. The faint drone of approaching aircraft grew in volume, and with the first crack of the guns came the high-pitched wail of the falling bombs.

More than a hundred aircraft let go their bomb loads through wispy cloud; an entirely wasted effort. Below them the docks lay empty.

The German battle fleet had left harbour two hours behind schedule, but by midnight thirty minutes had been snatched back by breakneck steaming. The night was very dark, with a clear canopy of stars shining brilliantly in their black setting. At sea level thin wisps of mist occasionally shrouded the ships as they turned the corner and approached the Channel entrance. Only the rush of water past each ship broke the stillness. They were a community cut off from the world by their Commander's strictly enforced orders for wireless silence.

Navigators plotted their progress along the route, while ashore German radar operators tracked them with some astonishment at their high speed through the water, then reckoned at 31 knots. Anxious eyes of lookouts strained into the misty murkiness of the night; the only friendly ships at sea were the marker boats lining the route at intervals. Any other black shapes would be British.

All crews were at action stations. On *Scharnhorst*'s bridge, Admiral Ciliax, a realist with no illusions about his chances of success, waited tensely for what he considered must be inevitable — the sound of a reconnaissance aircraft's engines. The British, he thought grimly, were too experienced in the business of waging war at sea to let him pass unnoticed.

His hopes would have soared had he known of events on the British side — events which were to develop more strangely hour by hour, minute by minute. He had, in fact, already passed through our third line of defence, the first air reconnaissance patrol — "Stopper". Time was being lost. We needed the earliest possible discovery of the enemy squadron to enable massed attacks to be quickly mounted and sustained until they were destroyed.

What happened then?

A glimpse at the possible answer is found in the logs of the three Coastal Command radar reconnaissance patrols which covered the enemy's dark passage.

At 6.30 pm...

The "Stopper" aircraft took off for the first of a series of dusk-to-dawn patrols between Brest and the tip of the Breton peninsula. His radar — one of the early sets — was designed to pick up surface vessels at sea up to a limited range. The night was black, and without the radar the crew would be "sightless".

At 7 pm...

The aircraft arrived in the patrol area about the same time as Luftwaffe night fighters took off to clear the air in advance of the Brest breakout. These fighters were under strict orders to avoid encounters with bomber forces and to concentrate by controlled directions on to reconnaissance patrols.

At 7.25 pm...

A Ju88 night "destroyer" fighter flew low under Bomber Command's evening raid on Brest and nearly collided with the "Stopper" aircraft. The indignant Luftwaffe pilot, who had not been warned by his controller on the ground of the Coastal Command patrol, set about trying to shoot down his enemy, who rapidly indulged in the necessary aerobatics to lose the fighter. For the duration of this encounter the "Stopper" crew switched off their radar.

After a few minutes the two aircraft succeeded in losing each other and the "Stopper" crew turned on the radar set again. Unfortunately, nothing happened, and all attempts to make it work proved fruitless.

Bomber Command's raid on Brest had started, and the "Stopper" crew could see the glow of bursting bombs and flares in the distance. It seemed unlikely to the pilot that the enemy ships would move at that moment, and, as he had been rendered "sightless", he decided to return to base.

At 8.40 pm...

The "Stopper" aircraft landed and technicians swarmed aboard to trace the radar fault. No relief plane was sent up to maintain the vigil and after forty minutes the cause of the failure was still a mystery. The crew were ordered to man another aircraft to resume the patrol, but this one refused to start. A further fifty minutes passed before the defect was found to be caused by what the records describe as "a damp, cloggy plug".

At 10.48 pm...

The aircraft reached the patrol area and "Stopper" resumed — an hour after the enemy had broken out from Brest to pass through the "Stopper" area. The patrol proved to be so much wasted effort, and it is nothing if not extraordinary that Coastal Command should have issued an urgent and accurate appraisal of the situation on the 8th and then permitted a gap of three hours — from 7.40 to 10.38 — in their patrol scheme during the critical days.

When the "Stopper" aircraft returned to base two hours later the crew were informed that the radar fault in their first aircraft had been traced to a blown fuse, caused by the untrained crew switching a "cold" set on to full power.

The next of Coastal Command's reconnaissance patrols was the "Line SE," timed to begin at 7.40 pm.

At 7.40 pm...

The "Line SE" aircraft arrived punctually at the patrol area. Almost immediately the crew discovered that the radar set had broken down. They searched vainly for the cause for nearly an hour. Eventually the pilot broke wireless silence to report the defect and his inability to see much below him without radar.

At 9.13 pm...

The aircraft was ordered to return home. Once again no relief aircraft was sent up and the "Line SE" was left unguarded. The enemy ships might well have been intercepted had the patrol been maintained. The fault to the radar was later found to be due to enemy jamming.

It is clear that no effective reconnaissance was carried out during this patrol, with its untimely and abrupt ending.

Meanwhile, photographs taken during an afternoon reconnaissance over Brest showed the ships to be out of dry dock and lying along fuelling wharves.

After breaking through this fourth line of defence the German ships were confronted by the last of the Coastal Command reconnaissance patrols — the "Habo" patrol.

This patrol was supposed to cover the area between Havre and Boulogne until 7.30 am. Instead it was brought to an end an hour early. No mysterious influence was at work this far up the Channel; neither was the enemy. The Brest ships reached the "Habo" line about an hour after the last aircraft on this patrol had left, having been ordered to make only two circuits of the area and then return — because of mist, and the station controller's fear of fog. Aircraft and crews were valuable, but so surely was the chance to sight the enemy.

Once again a gap had been left in the reconnaissance scheme. Had this patrol been maintained until dawn, it would more than likely have observed the enemy approaching Havre.

In this manner our defence lines stretching from Brest to Havre, and including a secret agent, a submarine and a series of reconnaissance patrols over the Channel, had been pierced by the enemy not through his own cleverness, but by misfortune.

Far to the east at 4 am a signal from Dover brought the naval forces to immediate readiness. The Swordfish at Manston were manned by crews waiting in the cockpits; one was already flying a patrol over the Straits in search of enemy coastal convoys. At Harwich the six destroyers raised steam; they could clear harbour in fifteen minutes if necessary.

"Operation Fuller" called for this emergency alert each morning on the assumption that the enemy would reach the Straits before dawn. After daylight the danger would be over and crews would revert to normal routines. In Admiral Ramsay's view the possibility of fighting a battle then would be remote indeed.

CHAPTER 6: THE WAR DIARY OF FEBRUARY 12TH, 1942

At 8.05 am...

Dawn in the English Channel — a grey, misty dawn with rain and broken cloud. The wind was moderate and the sea slight, although there was every chance that it would become rougher later. The German battle fleet had been at sea for little more than ten hours, covered more than 250 miles of the dash and successfully evaded five lines of defence: As far as could be judged by Admiral Ciliax, hunched beneath his greatcoat on the bridge of *Scharnhorst*, they were as yet undetected.

He stretched his long body slowly, relief pouring through his aching limbs. His gaunt face twisted into a humourless grin as he thought of the sleep he might enjoy when all this was over. The darkness had protected him; it would have been difficult for his ships to fight back had an attack been launched during the night. Now, with daylight, he could command a formidable fire-power on the surface and in the air. Although the critical moment of arrival in the Dover Straits had yet to come, the German admiral permitted himself the luxury of mild exultation.

Five miles to port the sea and sky met in a mist, and somewhere beyond, unseen, lay England — perhaps the British were unaware of his presence. For the minute he was content to sip the hot coffee and look forward to the arrival of the Luftwaffe "umbrella".

There were other reasons for Admiral Ciliax to rejoice. His plan to take advantage of the tidal stream rushing up Channel had worked so well that the fleet had snatched back most of the time lost during the delay in departure. He glanced at his watch. They were only fifteen minutes behind the planned timetable.

He was surprised also to find that despite the high speed, exceeding 30 knots through the water, maintained during most of the dark passage, the fleet had kept station without incident. Big ships and their sixteen escorting destroyers and E-boats were more or less precisely where they should be — no mean achievement for ships that had been idle for months.

Already powerful, the fleet would grow to nearly sixty ships when the twenty-four E-boats and cluster of gunboats being supplied by the Western Naval Command met him off Cap Gris Nez — a large enough force to drive a powerful wedge into the Straits.

At 8.25 am...

Wing Commander M. Jarvis, senior controller of the Radar Filter Room at Fighter Command headquarters, Stanmore, came on duty. Through him would filter the various radar sightings across the Channel made by the string of radar stations along the south-eastern coast. These were manned by RAF personnel with one exception — Newhaven, which was operated by the Canadian Army.

Wing Commander Jarvis examined a plot — as radar sighting reports were called — which he decided were aircraft circling somewhere off Le Havre. He thought this might be enemy aircraft escorting coastal shipping and informed No11 Group. He noticed reports of interference which were thought to be caused by atmospherics. This type of interference had been frequently experienced in recent days, and not much attention was accorded it by the Canadians.

The plot examined by Jarvis was, in fact, the Luftwaffe "umbrella" arriving over the battle squadron. The interference was the first move in Luftwaffe General Martini's plan to jam our radar to delay as long as possible discovery of the fleet's presence.

At 8.30 am...

The German Senior Officer of Escorts broke radio silence in accordance with instructions contained in "Cerberus" to inform the various German commands in France and at home of the fleet's position. In reply the Western Naval Command warned of a minefield laid by the Royal Navy the previous night and which lay across the route. Minesweepers were already at work.

Admiral Ciliax decided against making a detour. He would have to accept the risk and steam across it.

At 8.35 am...

Admiral Ramsay sent out a signal informing his forces that the critical "before-dawn" alert was ended. Ships were to revert to normal notice for steam, the Swordfish to resume their duties under the "Channel Stop" scheme of patrols.

The Ramsgate MTB flotilla had gone out the previous evening to attack a coastal convoy off Ostend. An enemy destroyer force had appeared, given them a bad mauling, and in the retreat three MTBs had gone ashore off South Foreland. Only three others remained. At Dover another MTB had developed engine trouble which would keep her out of action for several days.

There were no reserves in the "Fuller" plan; so a force which started out as twelve torpedo boats now consisted of eight.

At 8.45 am...

As part of the normal daily routine, Fighter Command sent out an early morning reconnaissance patrol covering an area between the mouth of the Somme and Ostend. This was known as the "Jim Crow" patrol, and it was designed to report the numbers and types of enemy shipping in the Channel. If the targets seemed worthwhile, the Command would generally organise a shipping strike called a "Roadstead" operation.

Admiral Ramsay would be informed, and once again it was up to him to decide if the "Jim Crow" reconnaissance reports contained anything which might merit sending his torpedo boats out. This was usual procedure and in no way connected with "Fuller" — indeed few but the most senior officers were aware that a Channel dash was even likely.

The "Jim Crow" this morning was undertaken by two Spitfires from Hawkinge, one of which flew straight to Boulogne, the westerly extremity of the patrol area. There it sighted E-boats leaving harbour and travelling south. Then the Spitfire flew to Berck, where another E-boat was seen steaming north. In accordance with his standing orders, which prohibited the use of wireless on these patrols, the pilot maintained radio silence and flew back home to report.

The second Spitfire reconnoitring between Cap Gris Nez and Ostend sighted eleven small vessels east of Zeebrugge. It also turned back to report. The pilot had seen, in fact, the beginnings of the horde of small vessels waiting to reinforce the battle fleet when it reached the Straits.

About this time the Duty Air Commodore at Stanmore rang through to No11 Group at Hornchurch and spoke to the Duty Controller. They discussed the radar reports of orbiting aircraft over the Channel, and the No11 Group Controller said that in his opinion "there's probably some sort of air-sea rescue operation going on out there, I should think".

At 9 am...

The transfer of Coastal Command's Beaufort squadron from Leuchars began. Fourteen aircraft took off for Coltishall, in East Anglia, on the first leg of their journey south, already delayed for two days by weather and administrative difficulties since first receiving the order to transfer on the 8th.

At 9.25 am...

Wing Commander Jarvis reported again to the Duty Air Commodore at Fighter Command headquarters plots from the Newhaven coastal stations showing what seemed to be two or three enemy aircraft orbiting over a section of the Channel. More interference was also reported.

When compared with the previous plots, the orbiting aircraft were making more than 20 knots up Channel. The Duty Air Commodore discussed this with No11 Group Duty Controller, and it was decided that the radar interference must be causing mistakes in the plot. No coastal ships slow enough to need aircraft protection could possibly steam at that sort of speed.

At 9.41 and 9.47 am...

Two more radar reports from coastal stations reached the Filter Room, both indicating two or more aircraft circling over the Channel south of Boulogne.

Radar experts held a conference on the meaning of these reports, but decided that the "atmospheric interference" was too bad for any true picture to be drawn of what the aircraft were doing.

At 9.59 am...

A fourth radar report of aircraft circling and of interference was received from the Fairlight Station and a further conference was held by the Filter Room staff. Although deliberate jamming was not unknown to them, they were misled by the intermittent character of the "interference" as described in the reports from various radar stations. Reports of aircraft circling over a small area were common enough, and more often than not were explained by enemy air-sea rescue operations or by individual enemy aircraft exercising and testing their guns. The conference again decided that any of these alternatives would explain the present radar reports.

At 10 am...

Wing Commander Jarvis had become worried. Instinct and training told him that something was wrong in the Channel. Continued plots of orbiting aircraft made it clear, despite constant interference, that surface vessels were making their way up Channel at a definite speed and on a northerly course.

He reported his fears to the Duty Air Commodore and to No11 Group — but Fighter Command was more concerned with mounting a shipping strike "Roadstead" operation against the E-boats reported by the early "Jim Crow" reconnaissance, and ordered a second of these reconnaissances to pin-point the enemy vessels. Once more No11 Group dismissed the radar plot as of no more interest than possibly enemy aircraft exercising.

At 10.16 am...

The RAF radar station at Beachy Head plotted two surface ships in the vicinity of Boulogne. They tried to telephone Dover to report the plot, but were unable to get through.

Further attempts on a secret "scrambler" line proved equally useless. Two minutes later another plot of these ships showed them moving on a defined course. A second try at contacting Dover by telephone failed.

At 10.20 am...

The second "Jim Crow" reconnaissance consisting of another two Spitfires took off from Hawkinge, one piloted by Squadron-Leader Oxspring and the other by Sergeant Beaumont.

Meanwhile a series of discussions had taken place by telephone between Admiral Ramsay, the Admiralty and the three Air Commands. It was generally agreed that there was little or no possibility of the Brest ships breaking port during the day. The next alert was set for four o'clock the following morning.

At 10.30 am...

Wing Commander Jarvis and his Filter Room staff discussed again the "atmospheric" interference, and Jarvis put forward the possibility that the enemy might be attempting to jam the coastal stations. Scientists were called in and Jarvis suggested to No11 Group that a special reconnaissance should be flown to check that the enemy jamming was not endeavouring to hide something in the Channel. This was turned down on the ground that Oxspring and Beaumont were already up and could be expected to return shortly.

Curiously, no one at Fighter Command headquarters or at No11 Group had seen fit to pass on the plots of orbiting aircraft to the Admiralty, where staff officers might have sensed the implications.

At Beachy Head radar station investigation of the defective telephone lines revealed an unexpected sidelight to the day's developments. Both the ordinary telephone and the secret "scrambler" were plugged into the same Post Office line — a discovery that would make an intelligence officer grow pale at the thought of how many private citizens in the area had lifted their telephones to hear Beachy Head and Dover discussing highly secret radar reports.

The radar operators now called Portsmouth naval command with a request that their two plots of enemy shipping be routed through to Dover.

At 10.33 am...

Group Captain Victor Beamish, famous Battle of Britain ace, was taking one of his "Beamish Special" jaunts over the Channel. These were "special" only because Beamish, senior staff officer to Air Vice-Marshal Leigh-Mallory, of No11 Group, should have been behind a desk instead of a joystick. No one, however, could keep Beamish away from his Spitfire for long, and rather than have him break the rules, Leigh-Mallory had allotted him an allowance of flights each week. Like a drug addict, Beamish had to be weaned away from flying in excess by a gradual decrease in the dosage.

Piloting another Spitfire was Wing Commander Boyd, also a Battle of Britain survivor, who had been assigned the unenviable task of keeping his senior officer out of trouble. This was regarded as a near to impossible duty, as Beamish used his allowance solely either to find the enemy in the air or impudently "beat up" his airfields in the hope of tempting him up.

The weather was reasonable, with the overcast breaking a little, the wind was still moderate and visibility remaining constant at five miles. Beamish knew of a possible Channel dash by the enemy, but on this morning both pilots were blithely unaware of the gathering climax below. They had just sighted a pair of Huns and, as Beamish described it later, "couldn't have cared less about Brest, battleships or breakout". With a joyful wave to Boyd, Beamish led the race into attack.

The Luftwaffe pilots cast hasty glances over their shoulders and retreated anxiously in the direction of Boulogne with the Spitfires close behind. Hunters and hunted lost height rapidly, and almost before they could do anything about it, Beamish and Boyd were streaking across the bows of the great German armada.

Both pilots lost interest in the Luftwaffe and gazed with open-mouthed amazement at the enemy fleet with creamy bow waves pouring over the foredecks of the proud battle cruisers and the long lines of escorts bouncing at high speed against the choppy seas. They turned in a steep banking movement and headed for home on a reverse course, pursued by the Luftwaffe "umbrella".

Fighter pilots were bound by Fighter Command's standing orders to maintain wireless silence. There were no exceptions to the rule. But here was an unforeseen circumstance, one which surely would never be repeated. One flick of the switch and Beamish's voice could boom out a warning to England of the enemy at her door.

With caution instilled by experience, Beamish was reluctant to disobey orders. With a wave to Boyd, he led the way back to base, preferring, perhaps unwisely, to obey orders rather than to break them.

Time was lost again, while on the ground the uneasy pattern of seemingly unrelated events was taking shape.

At 10.40 am...

The Beachy Head shipping plots were telephoned through to Dover from Portsmouth, and it was about then that Oxspring and Beaumont came down through the cloud fifteen miles west of Le Touquet to see a large number of ships directly below.

They also saw a formation of enemy fighters racing towards them, so they quickly nipped back into the cloud and with Oxspring leading headed home to report.

At 10.45 am...

The Beachy Head radar reports took a new significance when Fairlight Station telephoned Dover with a plot of about two ships also in the vicinity of Boulogne. This report reached Wing Commander J. "Bobby" Constable-Roberts, Air Liaison Officer on Admiral Ramsay's staff, who had been in constant touch with Fighter Command, No11 Group and Coastal Command's No16 Group.

He telephoned No11 Group immediately and informed them of the plot. He asked for a reconnaissance of the Boulogne area. No11 replied: "That's all right, Dover. We have been watching that one for some time."

The Beachy Head and Fairfight reports were the first indications Constable-Roberts had received of any large ships in the Channel; and he could see no reason why No11 Group should be better informed than anyone else. He cross-examined the Group's Staff Officer (Operations) and, as he had suspected, the officer was confusing these new shipping reports with the earlier ones concerned with orbiting aircraft.

Constable-Roberts pressed home the point that these ships could be "our friends coming up from the West" and again asked for a reconnaissance. The Group were content, however,

to reply that another "Jim Crow" was already in the air —
Oxspring and Beaumont — and their report could be expected
shortly. Taking a more serious view than the Fighter Group,
Constable-Roberts telephoned No16 Group, Coastal
Command, and made it clear that in his opinion there was
"something out there pretty important and it might be our
friends".

It was startlingly apparent that because of lethargy elsewhere,
Wing Commander Constable-Roberts emerges as the first
officer in the country to be alert to the possibility of a Brest
breakout. This officer not only recognised the danger, but did
his best to inspire the same sense of urgency in the other
Commands.

At 10.50 am...

Oxspring and Beaumont landed at Hawkinge. They reported
sighting a convoy of "about thirty to forty ships escorted by
five destroyers or E-boats". Sergeant Beaumont added that he
had seen a ship "with a tripod mast".

The interrogating officer looked excited.

"Thanks; that's just what we have been waiting for," he
announced.

The astonished Beaumont was then handed a book of
silhouettes of German warships.

"Could you recognise the ship you saw from these pictures,
do you think?" asked the interrogator.

Beaumont carefully turned the pages. His finger stabbed
suddenly at the etched outline of a German battleship.

"That looks like the mast I saw, sir," he said.

It was neither the *Scharnhorst*, *Gneisenau* nor *Prinz Eugen*.
Curiously, it seems that this identification was final. When the
report was sent through to Fighter Command, there was no

suggestion of an alert or putting "Fuller" into operation. Instead, the fact that Oxspring and Beaumont had seen a large convoy had the only effect of cancelling the previously ordered shipping strike and the issuing of fresh orders for a much larger "Roadstead" operation.

But an uneasy feeling was spreading through the various Commands.

At 11.05 am...

The news that a large convoy had been sighted off Boulogne and that a "Roadstead" operation, or shipping strike, was to be launched on a grander scale reached Dover. There was no mention of possible big warships or of one "with a tripod mast". Once again, however, Constable-Roberts recognised the possibilities and took the initiative.

With the reluctant approval of Admiral Ramsay, who was sceptical and inclined to wait for firmer evidence, the Air Liaison Officer telephoned Manston and had Eugene Esmonde called to the receiver.

"You had better get your chaps ready, Esmonde," he said evenly. "I think we might have something for you. There's nothing definite yet, but I've got a hunch it might well be the boys from Brest. Keep this line clear and I'll have you kept in the picture."

"How about bombing up?" replied Esmonde. "Shall I set the torpedoes deep?"

"Yes, you won't have any time when I give the word."

This was the first decisive step taken by the British forces — and a junior Wing Commander had taken it. Constable-Roberts next contacted No16 Group of Coastal Command at Thorney Island and suggested that the Beauforts on the way down from Leuchars and those at St Evall be warned. He felt keenly that they should be sent to Manston immediately, but it would have been outside his duties to suggest it.

At 11.09 am...

Half an hour after sighting and identifying the German battle fleet, Beamish and Boyd landed their Spitfires and raced to the nearest telephone. Cross-examination caused further delay, but eventually headquarters were satisfied and the telephones from No11 Group sent out the warning to the dazed Commands which had not at any time considered the enemy bold enough to attempt a daylight run through the Straits — the Brest ships were out; for the second time in history a great armada was approaching the Dover Straits, not to invade, but to escape.

The news that a night passage — on which "Fuller" and many private hopes rested — was an empty illusion struck through Whitehall with sickening suddenness; for the question to be faced was frighteningly clear — could our air and sea forces, perhaps sufficient to carry out the task allotted them under cover of darkness, possibly succeed in daylight against Germany's vastly superior strength?

Worse — the Admirals and the Air Marshals had but seconds to decide if they should send such slender forces to virtual death without regard to success or failure. From the most junior of them all upwards there was the conviction that these men would not survive, that, after all, their David might not have the necessary sling or a large enough pebble.

At 11.25 am...

Dover Command, most urgently affected of all, was the last to be informed. The news came by telephone from the Admiralty War Room. Immediately, Constable-Roberts asked

No11 Group for fighters to protect the Swordfish. A few minutes later he rang Esmonde at Manston and said:

"It's our Brest friends all right. Beamish has seen them off Boulogne. Stand by the phone and I'll get your orders soon."

Simultaneously, Victor Beamish rang Gleave from Kenley: "Fuller — get cracking, Tom, lad."

At 11.30 am...

At sea aboard *Scharnhorst*, Admiral Ciliax and his staff had lost some of their earlier confidence. It seemed impossible that they should have been at sea for nearly fourteen hours, the last four of these in daylight with visibility good, and escaped detection. Radar, or an unseen reconnaissance aircraft, must have reported their presence in the Channel; yet, if so, why had the British not appeared? This prolonged silence on the part of an enemy who could be relied upon to strike quickly and hold on tenaciously to an invader of the Channel struck an ominous chord throughout the German fleet.

Somewhere up ahead, thought Ciliax, a trap has been baited. He shrugged the fear aside; the operation had gone too far for him to do anything but sail into it.

Most nerve-racking incident of the voyage so far had been the crossing of the minefield reported that morning. By the time they arrived, minesweepers had swept eight mines, seven of which had been detonated, and cleared a gap 400 yards wide through what was thought to be the middle. The fleet had reduced speed to ten knots and steamed across the field astern of the minesweepers. Twenty tense minutes later they were in safe waters again. Full speed was ordered and the dash resumed.

At 11.40 am...

No11 Group controller informed Constable-Roberts by telephone that arrangements had been made for five fighter squadrons to provide close escort for the Swordfish torpedo bombers. Three more, he said, would attack the E-boat screens in advance of the MTB attack. Five minutes later, Admiral Ramsay signalled to Captain Pizey, leader of the Harwich destroyer flotilla:

Proceed in execution of previous instructions.

Fortunately, these ships had not reduced their period of notice for steam and, in fact, were already at sea off Harwich on anti-submarine exercises.

The lack of any but the loosest co-ordination between Commands came to the fore when No16 Group's senior staff officer telephoned Constable-Roberts with a request that he delay the Swordfish takeoff in order that a combined attack could be made with the Beaufort torpedo bombers. In such an overwhelming emergency, Constable-Roberts acted with remarkable logic. He at once replied that this was impossible and gave his reasons as:

> 1. It was important to try to cripple the enemy as quickly as possible where it would be reasonable to expect larger surface units to destroy him.
> 2. To have attacked with the Beauforts would have meant separate fighter escorts, as the Swordfish could fly at not more than 90 knots, while the Beauforts would have extreme difficulty in flying at less than 150 knots. For the Swordfish it would have meant a two and a half hours' flight under constant enemy fighter attack to reach the enemy ships.
> 3. Casualties were a foregone conclusion, and there was more chance of picking up survivors if the battle took place within a few miles of our shores.

Having dealt with this tactical problem at short notice, he was ordered to telephone No11 Group and pass on the probable course and speed of the MTBs which were about to leave harbour. Fighter cover was promised within ten minutes.

Inside this period the torpedo boats sailed from Dover and raced across the Straits to attack. Two motor gun boats which had recently arrived at Dover to act as cover for the MTBs were not yet ready to sail. And at 11.55 am Sir Philip Joubert was informed that his Leuchars Beauforts had landed at Coltishall. He recalls that his feelings were tense at this stage because there were no torpedo facilities at this field.

At 12.00 am...

There was still no sign of the British forces. Ciliax's fear of a trap gave way to the faintest hope that he might escape without a fight, as the battle squadron reached the Straits of Dover. A few minutes later and they were joined by the Cap Gris Nez E-boat flotillas and the Cap itself lay broad on the starboard beam — the narrowest part of the Straits had been breached.

A surge of buoyancy swept through the German crews. They had sailed 360 miles through hitherto forbidden waters; only another 200 miles lay between them and the safety of home waters.

Admiral Ciliax, carrying the tremendous burden of responsibility and knowing full well that his career was irrevocably tied to the success or failure of the operation, remained subdued. He would not openly rejoice until the last stretch lay astern of his flagship.

Even had he been destroyed at that moment, he would still have been the only German commander to sail the entire length of the English Channel unmolested.

Eighteen miles separated the fleet from the cliffs of Dover, hidden in the thin rain-mist lying on the sea. Which would come first — the attack from the air, or from the sea? There was one move he could make which might confuse his enemy. He ordered his yeoman of signals:

"Tell the port side screens to make smoke," and, turning to his Chief of Staff, grinned: "A decent smokescreen should give the English something to think about."

At 12.10 pm...

Dover Command informed the Corps of Coastal Artillery, who manned the Dover batteries, of the developing situation. There was little hope of long-range gunfire being of much help, as the enemy ships could not be seen through the misty weather aggravated by the smokescreens. The enemy radar jamming had been stepped up to the extent that it was becoming impossible to keep a readable plot.

There was still no accurate report of the position, course and speed of the enemy fleet, and Admiral Ramsay waited impatiently for his MTBs to make their contact signal.

Then No11 Group controller rang Constable-Roberts with a formal request that Dover confirm that fighter escort provision for the Swordfish attack would be adequate. Constable-Roberts told the controller to check with Esmonde. This was done immediately, and with the assurance that five squadrons would rendezvous with him over Manston, Esmonde decided to take off. It was agreed between Esmonde and No11 Group that three of these squadrons from Biggin Hill should act as top cover, while two from Hornchurch would stay close to the Swordfish and attack flak ships. Time fixed for the rendezvous was 12.25 pm.

At 12.15 pm...

There was still no accurate information about the enemy's movements. No fighter reconnaissance aircraft had been sent out, although it was nearly an hour since Beamish had vaguely reported: *They are out there somewhere off Boulogne.* The Dover torpedo boats had not yet made contact. Radar plots were still being jammed and at Dover there was some doubt of their accuracy. The Navy preferred to wait for a "sighting report".

However, it was now that Admiral Ramsay made his dramatic signal to the Admiralty:

> *All measures prepared in my Command to counter the enemy move have been put into operation.*

The German battle fleet had already crossed the Dover-Calais line and were through the Straits of Dover. The Channel dash was to be challenged in the Narrow Sea.

At 12.18 pm...

The Armed Forces formally engaged the enemy for the first time. The Dover batteries opened fire and a plume of spray leapt upwards briefly more than a mile to port of the nearest German escort. But the enemy was fast drawing out of range — he was through the danger point where his ships would have been less than two miles from the French coast and his freedom of movement reduced to practically nil by shallow water and sandbanks to one side, and minefields to the other. These conditions would prevail up the Belgian and Dutch coasts, but never to the same restrictive extent as in the Straits.

The two MGBs sailed from Dover in an attempt to engage the outer E-boat screen so that the MTBs would have a chance to break through.

At 12.23 pm...

Lieutenant-Commander E. N. Pumphrey, leader of the MTBs, raced towards several dull shapes about five miles ahead. Their contours became clearer as the distance closed, and with his boats roaring behind him he turned on a parallel course to the E-boats, which he rightly decided were part of the enemy outer screen. Wrongly, he thought they were the stern section, but he soon discovered his mistake when suddenly the great shapes of the battle cruisers emerged from the smokescreen laid by destroyers. He signalled the traditional naval "enemy sighted" report, including an accurate estimate of his position and the enemy's course and speed.

It reached Dover in time to be transmitted to the Ramsgate torpedo boats which had just moved away from the jetty and were proceeding out of harbour. It was also sent to Eugene Esmonde, who was impatiently waiting for the fighters due to give him protection. Without them it was doubtful if he would be permitted to take off, or whether, as a volunteer, he would care to continue the operation.

At 12.45 pm...

The Dover batteries ceased firing, having sent thirty-three rounds of 9-inch shells hurtling after the retreating enemy. According to German reports none was closer than the first.

The Battle of the Narrow Sea had opened. The great shore batteries had failed, but ready to pounce were the MTBs and the Swordfish of the Fleet Air Arm; Bomber and Coastal Command were massing their forces, and squadrons of Spitfires and Hurricanes were streaking up to challenge the Luftwaffe, its full strength of nearly 300 aircraft now thrown in to form a vast "umbrella" over the entire battle fleet, which had snowballed to about sixty ships of all sizes. The Luftwaffe bombers were already taking off in readiness to dive-bomb the attacking sea forces.

Little more than four hours of daylight remained.

CHAPTER 7: THE BATTLE OF THE NARROW SEA

Lying low over the Narrow Sea between Ostend and the south-east corner of England, the slightly breaking, overcast cloud threatened to close down visibility. But the wind was not yet strong enough to whip the seas into the hard corrugations which could rip through the thin wooden hulls of torpedo boats racing at full speed.

The five Dover MTBs led by *221*, with Lieutenant-Commander Pumphrey in command, steamed at 36 knots on a parallel course to the enemy fleet's port outer screen of E-boats. Slightly astern and two miles on *221*'s starboard quarter the great shadowy shapes of the enemy heavy ships emerged from the long black layer of smoke laid by attendant destroyers — smoke that was now rising in the thin, wispy curtain from the sea to the clouds behind which the main fleet had passed through the Straits.

On either side of the big ships were sandbanks and minefields, but careful planning and the "blitz" minesweeping operation had provided a route three miles wide up the Belgian and Dutch coasts. Every few miles marker boats anchored on the sidelines acting as beacons to eventual safety.

The distance between the opposing lines of E-boats and MTBs closed to 1000 yards' and the continuous chatter of light guns sent an archway of red tracers floating across the watery no man's land. The British boats were not designed to fight running gun battles; they were equipped only to pierce the screen, deliver their torpedo blows against the main units and retire — if possible.

Dismayed at the mischance which had delayed the departure of the Dover gunboats, Pumphrey glanced anxiously upwards for some sign that the fighter escorts were on their way to engage the E-boats. Either force would have provided the necessary distraction to enable him to draw ahead of the enemy, pass across the screen's bows and surge down inside to make a head-on attack against *Scharnhorst* first. His boats would be on their own after that.

221 was pushing across the surface like a speedboat, stern well down below her wake, bows inclined upwards and the sea beating a shuddering tattoo against her bottom. The roar of the triple aero engines drowned the sound of guns. While he was so close to the E-boats there was little danger from the big ships; once through the screen and their main armament would tear his formation apart.

Wedged behind the compass on *221*'s bridge he looked astern to check that the flotilla were keeping up. There was *219* with Arnold-Foster in command, a young RNVR sub-lieutenant who was rapidly becoming an operational veteran; then came Gamble with *45* — a slightly older lieutenant who already held the Distinguished Service Cross; the Dominions were represented by the Australian, Saunders, in *44*, and Tony Law from Canada followed up the rear in *48*.

Pumphrey's attention was drawn abruptly back to the enemy by the whump of light shells pumping into *221*'s hull. He glanced at the E-boats, noticed they were picking up speed, and felt a sudden wave of frustration as it quickly became apparent that he would not have sufficient reserve to draw ahead to cross their bows.

Without warning, his engines faltered and died away, the sudden drop in speed pulling *221*'s bows down into the water. He pulled frantically at controls while the boats astern slowed up to maintain formation. As mysteriously as they had stopped the engines throbbed to life again. But the line of E-boats was passing ahead and Pumphrey, with quick decision, abandoned his earlier policy and turned *221* towards them in an attempt to crash his way through the screen.

Almost immediately his engines failed again and *221*'s speed dropped to 15 knots. Pumphrey ordered his flotilla to attack independently just as the first German fighters swooped low to strafe their decks. Caught between accurate, effective E-boat fire and constant air strafing, the MTBs split up to make individual attacks.

Pumphrey decided that his best — if not only — course was to allow the enemy screen to pass down his starboard beam, wait until the heavy ships came abreast of him and then turn in to fire at a range of about two miles. By doing so he would expose his crippled boat to concentrated fire from not only the E-boats and fighters but from either the large destroyer inner screen or the battle cruisers.

Scharnhorst came into his sights first. Pumphrey pointed *221*'s nose at her as he quickly estimated the target's speed and calculated the range. His gunners shouted, and he turned to see two E-boats standing off 800 yards away with guns winking brightly at him. He chose to ignore this danger and turned his attention back to *Scharnhorst*. His hand jerked down the firing lever, two long steel torpedoes hurtled from the bows, splashed into the sea and sped towards the target, their tracks hidden in the white-topped waves.

While Pumphrey waited tensely for the hit, his gunners fought back at the attacking E-boats. A thunder of sound rolled across the battlefield and Pumphrey's heart leapt with sudden joy. But it was the first cannonade from the *Scharnhorst*'s heavy guns laying a barrage ahead of him. Cordite smoke billowed from the long muzzles of the enemy guns, hiding the tall superstructure as well as any smokescreen and adding to the confusion of smoke and cloud drifting over the fleet.

Pumphrey glanced at his watch. The torpedoes had missed. Disappointed, he turned his boat away from the battle.

Well ahead, the rest of his flotilla were desperately trying to reach attacking positions. *219* and *48* were beaten back by the E-boat screen and then singled out for special attention by a swarm of fighters. Dodging and twisting, they fought back to within 400 yards of the screen and launched their torpedoes at *Scharnhorst* from a range of about 5000 yards. There was no time to wait for results. Subjected to vicious crossfires, Arnold-Foster of *219* and Tony Law of *48* worked their way back to the deepfield. The Germans switched their fire to Gamble in *45*.

He was trying to pass under the stern of the last E-boat in line when the destroyer *Friedrich Ihn* moved across to block his sights. He altered course to pass down the outside of the screen before turning to make a run through a gauntlet of fire between the two centre E-boats. It was a brave, defiant attack. His bullet-torn boat shuddered under the impact of shells and fighter cannon-fire, but he held his course and reached the gap.

E-boat fire poured into the little *45* as she pointed her nose at *Prinz Eugen*, steadied under the helm and then bounced on the waves as her torpedoes left the tubes. Gamble had not fired a minute too soon. The menacing bows of the *Friedrich Ihn*, which had raced up the inside of the screen to intercept his breakthrough, reared above. Her guns cracked down and shell splashes poured over the boat. Gamble juggled fiercely with the controls, turned her away from the enemy and ran the gauntlet back again to safety. But not before he had seen his torpedoes misfire and sink — a valiant failure.

He was still in trouble. The *Friedrich Ihn* burst through the E-boats and charged after him. Coaxing the last effort from his engines, Gamble was able to maintain his lead to make a twisting evasive retreat to the north. Fuel was becoming an urgent problem when suddenly the two Dover MGBs raced between Gamble and the destroyer with light armament blasting and a trail of smoke pouring out behind them. Behind the protection of the smokescreen he was able to alter course and double back towards Dover. The *Friedrich Ihn*, not liking the needling fire of the new arrivals, turned back towards the battlefield.

Meanwhile the fifth boat, *44*, had dropped well astern with engine trouble. Now, her damage repaired, she caught up with the screen again and, despite constant air attacks, moved inside a little behind the last E-boat. Taking advantage of a lull in the fighter strafing and the momentary surprise of the E-boat crew at such an impudent manoeuvre, Saunders fired his torpedoes at *Prinz Eugen* from a range of about 3000 yards.

The few seconds waiting to see if the torpedoes were running straight were interrupted abruptly by the arrival of the destroyer *Herman Schoemann*, which opened fire on *44* at less than half a mile. There was no rewarding explosion of torpedoes hitting the German cruiser, so *44* turned to make good her retreat. The destroyer moved across to intercept and found herself caught in a crossfire from the two MGBs which had sneaked up from astern.

Now they sped between *44* and her pursuer. The Senior Officer, Lieutenant P. F. S. Gould, said in his report later:

"We sighted the MTBs withdrawing towards the English coast in scattered formation and under fire from a large destroyer. I placed the MGBs between the destroyer and the MTBs and fought a gun duel with it and enemy fighters while the MTBs made good their escape — the last one being chased until the enemy was more than ten miles from his coast.

"The battle was fought at 35 knots and the enemy fire was unpleasantly accurate.

"It was gratifying to know that having left harbour later than the MTBs we were able to adequately assist their withdrawal intact."

Covered by the gunboats, Saunders dropped astern of the quickly moving battleground, from where the roar of heavy barrages from the battle cruisers was almost continuous now. The Luftwaffe turned away from the retreating torpedo boats and mustered over the battle fleet. Esmonde's Swordfish were skimming in to the attack.

Saunders thought it likely that the Swordfish crews might need help when — not if — shot down. He decided to wait and watch in the sidelines. It was a wise decision, for little help was forthcoming from Ramsgate. These three MTBs sailed half an hour after the Dover flotilla and soon met enemy destroyers and E-boats.

The leader, Lieutenant D. J. Long, in *32*, thought these ships must be screening the port-bow position from the battle squadron and manoeuvred to be in firing position when the big ships reached him.

However, it soon became clear that the reverse was the case — he had crossed astern of the rear escorts, and the principal targets were now several miles ahead. The problem of how to reach the enemy was settled for him when all three boats developed engine trouble. This, in addition to rapidly deteriorating weather and rising sea, made it impossible to catch up. Long led his boats back into harbour.

It is unlikely that these three would have made any difference to the outcome. From the beginning the MTBs had faced a wall of nearly thirty E-boats backed up by the inner screen of gunboats and destroyers. Outnumbered and outgunned, they had been fortunate in pressing home their attacks to the extent that they were able to fire torpedoes.

The first battle for control of the Narrow Sea had been fought and lost — not by the men who went into action with magnificent courage, but by impossible odds.

At Dover, Admiral Ramsay was waiting for the first of the boats to return and report the state of the battle; he was also aflame with anger at another tragic mistake — the Swordfish takeoff on a mission from which there could be no return. The story began when the squadron transferred from Lee-on-Solent to Kent.

CHAPTER 8: CALCULATED SUICIDE

No825 Squadron's Swordfish landed at Manston in a blizzard. They were armed with torpedoes and dispersed for takeoff. Wing Commander Tom Gleave had already assigned quarters for officers and men, and the RAF mess welcomed their naval opposites as guests. That evening Gleave invited Esmonde to join him for discussions on the plan to incorporate 825 in "Fuller", while at the same time they would carry out "Channel Stop" patrols over the Straits. Only Esmonde knew that a dash was expected any day. Manston had not been warned of this.

Gleave, once wide-shouldered and stocky with a square blunt face under straight dark hair, was a fighter veteran with a distinguished Battle of Britain record and the reputation of being a man not easily impressed. His fast, clipped speech had on occasion whipped senior and junior officers with magnificent impartiality. Then he had gone down in a blazing Hurricane; later, he became a patient of the great McIndoe, plastic surgeon by choice to the RAF during the war. After one year and a dozen operations, Tom Gleave was restored sufficiently to resume active duty with new eyelids, a new nose and skin grafted on his burned legs; a skeleton who wore loose battledress and a greatcoat to give him shape.[8]

It was the first time that Tom Gleave had met the young naval officer whose reputation as a flier ranked with the finest in the country; curiosity mingled with admiration when he recognised in the wiry, round-faced Esmonde the same qualities of leadership and ability to inspire others that he had

---

[8] Group Captain Gleave received more "beauty treatment" later, and today is more like his pre-war self with weight around 13½ stone.

known in another splendid pilot — Guy Gibson of Bomber Command.

Both men were unexpectedly small, yet radiated a quiet confidence and strength of will and character which lifted them above the ordinary into the realms where legends are born. Both had a tremendous capacity for sheer hard work; both absorbed experience gained by taking risks before expecting others to follow suit.

When new types of bombs or torpedoes needed testing it was Esmonde who accepted the responsibility as a matter of course: later it was Gibson who blazed the trail for his dam busters to follow in their hazardous operation.[9]

Both men had an abundance of personal charm, which in relaxed moments gave them not only the professional respect of their men, but friendship also. In consequence, they imparted confidence even at the most inconsequential times.

Gleave was under no false impression of the sort of man who would be required to lead the attack on the German battle squadron should it venture up the Channel; under Esmonde's spell he sensed that no other would be better. He found it easy to like Esmonde.

When he had volunteered his squadron for the attack, Esmonde had been told it would be certain to take place in the dark hours. Now he worked out with Gleave a training programme in low-level torpedo attack at night. His plan was to attack from ahead of the enemy formation with his Swordfish flying in the shape of a crescent, fanning out near the dropping point so that one flight of three would fire from the port side and the other flight from the starboard. This had the advantage of making their approach from an angle at which

---

[9] Guy Gibson, VC, led 617 Squadron on the famous raid described vividly in Paul Brickhill's book *The Dam Busters* (also a PAN book).

the enemy's maximum fire would be reduced to the for'ard guns alone while dividing the attention of night fighters.

Gleave promised to supply night fighters to drop flares over the targets throughout the attack period.

Next morning Manston was covered in thick, frosty drifts of snow. The maintenance crews from Lee-on-Solent arrived in lorries under Edgar Lee.[10] The aircraft were dug from their dispersal points and the training programme began without waste of time. The squadron's gunner (T) was desperately sick, but refused to be moved to hospital. Instead, throughout the intense training activity he serviced the torpedoes day and night until he collapsed and was hurried away from Manston unconscious.

One night during the first week Esmonde called his crews to a hut placed to one side of the main buildings which Gleave had loaned him as a crew room. At this conference he said:

"The possibility that the Brest ships will sail up Channel is not so much a theory now as a certainty. We have volunteered for the job of stopping them, and that is why you are here being trained round the clock. When the time to attack comes, I want you to take off without further need of orders.

"I am going to pass round slips of papers on which the names of the targets and my plan of attack are written. Commit the lot to memory, and before we leave here I want each slip burned.

"This is secret and there will be no discussions or talking about it. If Jerry knew that we were here and the purpose for which we are here, then he would take measures to either stop us or even abandon his Channel route."

---

[10] Lee was seconded to Gibson's squadron in Bomber Command after the *Scharnhorst* attack and recalls his astonishment at Gibson's physical resemblance to Esmonde.

There were seven pilots and six Swordfish. Before leaving the crew room, the two junior pilots tossed a coin for the right to fly the mission. Sub-Lieutenant Peter Bligh called and won. Sub-Lieutenant Bennett was to remain on the ground at Manston.

After this, Esmonde wrote his last letter to Drominagh, where his mother had been stricken with arthritis.

"When I was last in Dublin, mother, I bought a wheel-chair, and it is there any time you would like it. It is a light one you could use very satisfactorily ... it is only being garaged, so you might as well try it out."

When the critical days had passed he would be due for leave, and planned to pick up the chair and arrive with it at Drominagh. Perhaps a presentiment of what lay ahead made him write this letter so that his mother could enjoy the gardens of Drominagh should he be unable to be there himself.

On February 11th Esmonde drove to Margate and caught a train to London. He had not liked leaving his squadron but had been assured that it was a justifiable risk — he was to attend an investiture at Buckingham Palace to receive his Distinguished Service Order awarded for the *Bismarck* operation. In his pocket was a copy of the *London Gazette* announcing that he had been "mentioned in dispatches" for services while in *Ark Royal*.

Never one of the swiftest railway services in Britain, in wartime the Margate train crawled to London, arriving an hour late. Eugene had hoped to call at the Admiralty before the Palace ceremony to discuss the Channel operation with Admiral Power.

However, he had time only to change at his hotel, put on his sword and set off for the Palace. During the ceremony he sat in the front row of chairs facing the raised dais on which the late King George VI stood behind a green-topped table. Beside him was Queen Elizabeth, now the Queen Mother.

The Naval Aide called out:

"Lieutenant-Commander (A) Eugene Esmonde, please."

He stood stiffly before the King, whose warm smile of pleasure gave deep sincerity to the formalities which must follow and enriched the decoration itself with a memorable quality. Excited and proud, Eugene heard the quietly spoken words, "... and although I present you with this award, it is really given by all my peoples who are grateful for the inestimable value of your unselfish service to our country and our cause. My congratulations, and may I say thank you personally."

That evening he returned to Manston, where a mild and brief celebration had been prepared by the RAF and his own crews. It ended early and the crews dispersed to their cabins; at four o'clock in the morning they would be called to stand by their aircraft at fifteen minutes' notice for takeoff. This was Admiral Ramsay's alert for the pre-dawn danger period.

They mustered in the crew room, where ground staff were already waiting with hot coffee. The Swordfish had been moved to the take-off positions. The crews huddled down in chairs to while away the early morning hours. In one corner Edgar Lee and Esmonde swapped stories of the *Ark Royal*, in which they had met, and argued about tactics in the air, Lee voicing his doubts about the sanity of some pilots for whom he had been observer.

Esmonde told with feeling of a day in the Med when he had taken off from the *Ark Royal* to deliver a torpedo attack against an Italian battle squadron retreating at 30 knots from Corsican waters. His Swordfish had to battle against a 50-knot head wind and with a top speed of 90 knots was catching up at only

10 knots. When they came in sight the Swordfish overtook so slowly they presented almost stationary targets to the Italian gunners. "I'll never attack a retreating enemy again in those string bags," he said ruefully.

It was a typical stand-by scene, repeated in commands throughout the country, where emergencies of one sort or another were a nightly occasion. It ended in the same way — no call to action except a gallop to the mess for breakfast. Nothing about the morning of the 12th at Manston differed from any other morning since they had arrived.

After breakfast there was the usual gathering in the crew room, where duties for the day were listed on a notice-board. One of the more operationally experienced crews with Swordfish *W-5983* was down to fly a practice torpedo flight in the morning. The pilot, Sub-Lieutenant Brian Rose, had been with the squadron in the *Ark Royal*; his observer was Edgar Lee, and the *Bismarck* veteran, Leading Airman Johnson, was air gunner.

At ten o'clock they took off and vanished in the direction of Deal Bay, where they would exercise low flying in a series of dummy runs. Off-duty crews returned to their quarters; Esmonde joined his ground staff for a check over the torpedo armament in preparation for another of his everlasting struggles with the supply people at Lee-on-Solent. He thought bitterly that if the squadron could not be brought to full strength, at least what was left of it should be adequately supplied.

His rude notions of what fate would be best for those he called the "red-tape boys" ended abruptly when a messenger came rushing down the runway in a bent and scratched Morris Minor to shout:

"Dover wants you on the phone urgently, sir."

The little car leaned heavily on the remains of its springs as the driver swerved to a stop. Esmonde jumped in and two minutes later raced to operations control-room telephone. It was Constable-Roberts with the first warning that something was wrong in the Channel.

The bright eyes narrowed and the taut face took on the eager look of a frightened bird. He rested the receiver on a table and called out to the controller:

"Keep this line clear for me, will you? Dover thinks there might be a target for us."

The alarm from the Fleet Air Arm crews rang out as he quickly examined operational reports of weather and activity over the Channel. One by one the pilots, observers and gunners raced to the crew room. The control room came alive as messages were sent for Gleave, who was inspecting hangars on the other side of the field. The controller plugged a spare telephone into the Dover line to keep himself informed.

Wing Commander Gleave arrived in the "Stationmaster's wagon", an old Ford V8 given to slow rolls on corners. He joined Esmonde beside the telephone. Both were sceptical that it could be the heavy ships from Brest until the sickening realisation that perhaps it was, that possibly all expert opinion that the ships would not attempt to run the Dover gauntlet by day was wrong, drove every other thought from Esmonde's mind.

"What if it is?" he muttered almost inaudibly. And to the listening Gleave it was more a prayer than a question. There could be no reply; both men knew that if Constable-Roberts proved right, the Swordfish crews would fly to suicide.

Gleave left the naval officer alone and returned to his office, where he would be needed if "Fuller" was ordered into operation. Behind him the control room was subdued, the quiet broken only by the occasional crackling reports of pilots on test flights above the field. Esmonde sat wrapped in his own thoughts by the telephone.

At 11.30 the voice of Constable-Roberts snapped him back to life:

"It's the Brest boys all right. Beamish has seen them off Boulogne..."

Esmonde listened to the rest automatically, his mind filled with the recognisable anguish of a man faced with making an impossible decision — he had volunteered the squadron, therefore he had the right to refuse to fly. If he exercised this right he need never be ashamed, for the conditions were vastly changed from those which applied when volunteers were requested. It had been a night attack then, one in which there would have been the satisfying cloak of darkness to protect them.

It is probable that as he struggled to make his choice the boyhood principles with which he had been imbued at Drominagh came to his assistance. In everything he had done, in all his pursuits in the woodlands of Tipperary and on the sometimes placid, often stormy waters of Lough Derg, he had acquired little by little the meaning of duty — duty to family, duty to the community, duty to country and duty to himself. Above all, the performance of duty, no matter what the cost.

Now the cost would be high; the lives of seventeen men whom he had trained and watched grow prematurely old rested on his decision. The controller had listened to Constable-Roberts and saw the signs of the inward conflict reflected in the discernible greyness creeping over Esmonde's face. An experienced officer, he was shocked at the thought of the "stringbag squadron" challenging a battle fleet.

The courage of the man from Tipperary was not in doubt; nor was there any unwillingness to face the danger in the Channel. For himself there was no self-pity, and the crisis that had been reached was the natural result of the sense of a new vocation he had found two years before while serving in *Furious*.

"I can think of no greater honour," he had written, "nor a better way of passing into Eternity than in the cause for which the Allies are fighting this war."

Nothing had happened to change this — the time had come, and he knew it. There remained, however, the inward conflict clearly etched on his face that his crews, so young that the oldest was twenty-four, would have to fly with him into the holocaust that awaited them in the Channel.

Memories of Drominagh stirred then; memories of the great brooding house on the lakeside with its walls carrying the symbols of the family tradition — Colonel John Esmonde, VC, the other John who had commanded the frigate, *Lion*, Geoffrey, his older half brother who had died on the field at Ypres in the war before this one. Each of these had performed their duty, no matter what the cost.

For more than an half an hour he stood, grey, drawn and silent beside the telephone.

A voice spluttered into the receiver. Slowly he bent down to listen.

"Is that Lieutenant-Commander Esmonde?"

"Speaking."

"This is No11 Fighter Group here. Dover has asked us to give you fighter cover. We intend putting in the Biggin Hill Wing of three squadrons as top cover and the Hornchurch Wing of two squadrons will give you close escort and beat up the flack ships for you. Is that all right?"

The dazed look left Esmonde's eyes and he came alert. With good fighter escort there was just a chance that some of his crews would get back alive.

"That sounds fine. But tell your chaps to keep a close watch on us. The Luftwaffe will be up in strength and we will be just their meat."

"Right. The orders have gone out. Both Wings have been told to rendezvous with you over Manston. What time will you take off?"

Esmonde glanced at his watch. "Tell them to get here by 12.25, and for the love of heaven get them here on time."

"Got it." The line went dead.

He was unable to leave the phone until Dover confirmed that he should attack and reported the position, course and speed of the enemy. A message was sent to the crew room for all pilots and observers to report to him in the control room.

The decision was made. His duty was to attack the enemy and pray that the price would not be paid in full.

Constable-Roberts reached him from Dover again.

"Have No11 Group arranged escort for you yet?"

Esmonde replied crisply:

"Yes, they are giving us five squadrons for top cover and close escort. That's all they've got, and it should do the trick if they stay close."

"The Admiral wants to know how you feel about going in — he wants it to be your decision."

There was a slight pause before Esmonde replied with quiet humour:

"Yes, the squadron is going in, but tell the Old Man we ain't bloody heroes and not to expect miracles. Where is Jerry? What's his speed?"

"We don't know yet, old boy. Beamish said off Boulogne, but that was nearly an hour ago. Our MTBs are going in any minute and we should get a sighting report almost immediately."

"Well, I've arranged with No11 Group that I'll meet the fighter escorts here at 12.25. So don't keep us waiting."

"O.K. Stand by the phone. And Esmonde..."

"Yes."

It was Constable-Roberts who paused this time. Then he blurted: "Just want to say best of luck, old boy, and give the blighters bloody hell for me too." The voice died away.

Eugene Esmonde turned from the telephone to face his officers for the last time. The controller recalls the shock he experienced when he saw the usually tanned, bright-eyed face. Now he looked at "a man torn apart inside". Esmonde's eyes flickered over each in turn.

"The balloon's gone up," he said in his normal incisive manner, "and I want to say now how sorry I am that you were not warned that a day attack might be possible. I accept responsibility for that. It was my job to see that you were ready for this party."

His bleak stare silenced the angry ripples of denial.

"In a few minutes we will be going in. Forget all you have been told of the night-attack plan. We will attack in sub-flights in line astern, height fifty feet. Object: to hit and thereby slow down any one or all of the big ships.

"Thompson" — he turned to face a slimly-built, fair lieutenant wearing the straight gold rings of a regular officer — "you take the second flight and follow behind me. Keep about a thousand yards between us. That way we will divide their flak fire and with any luck we can draw some of it away from you.

"We will have plenty of fighter cover both on top and as close escort, so you won't have to worry too much about enemy fighters." Relief sighed through the room. "Once over the escorting screens, probably destroyers and E-boats, you can attack independently. Pick your target as the nearest to your most convenient dropping point — but make sure it is either *Scharnhorst*, *Gneisenau* or *Prinz Eugen*.

"We want to hit those ships where it will hurt most. If we do we will pay off old scores for the entire Fleet Air Arm — when things get bad, remember the eight Skuas shot down by *Scharnhorst* at Trondheim in 1940 and the two Swordfish knocked out by *Gneisenau* a few weeks afterwards." He grinned suddenly. "And if that doesn't help, remember your own necks.

"Now get to your aircraft, warm up and stand by."

The telephone crackled as Constable-Roberts came on the line.

"They are about ten miles north-east of the Straits going at 21 knots. The Admiral says it is O.K. to go if you are satisfied with the fighter escort."

The crews left the room in a rush. No questions were necessary; in the triple cockpits of the Swordfish a wave of the leader's hand could change the course of a battle. Esmonde was about to follow his crews when the telephone came to life again. It was No11 Group.

"We have just been told that some of your fighter escort might be a little late at the rendezvous."

The inward struggle started up again.

"How late?"

"A few minutes."

"Right. We are taking off at 12.25. Tell your chaps not to be later than two minutes. I'll orbit out to the coast. Will that do?"

"Yes, that's O.K. They mentioned two minutes' delay. That will do fine."

Esmonde slammed down the receiver and hurried out.

Just then Brian Rose landed *W-5983* and, leaving his gunner to check the firing equipment, walked with Lee to the crew room, where they changed and headed for the mess. The squadron roared past in a lorry.

"The balloon's gone up, you chaps," came a shout. "Better get cracking."

The pair raced back to the crew room to find Esmonde already putting on his kit.

"The Brest ships have had the cheek to try it out at last. We're going out to deal with them. Fly at fifty feet close astern of me; attack independently once we are over the screen and make your own way home."

He led the way out and the three dashed to their aircraft parked near the Margate road. It was 12.15 pm — and there was no sign of the fighter escort.

As they rushed across the field, Gleave, who was running along the road cutting across the field, altered direction to intercept Esmonde and wish him luck. The look on the face of the preoccupied naval officer pulled him up in his tracks.

"It was the face of a man already dead," he recalls. "I had always known him as a vital man, alive and eager for anything. Now his eyes were dulled, his face grey, almost haggard. The sort of vacant, lifeless face you read about but never expect to see. He barely recognised me, although his mouth twitched automatically into the semblance of a grin and an arm lifted in a vague wave. It shocked me as nothing had done before nor has done since." He walked past Gleave, a small figure in dark blue wearing an orange-coloured Mae West and an unstrapped flying helmet with the R/T leads dangling round his legs.

Esmonde's observer, Lieutenant W. H. Williams, RN, and his gunner, Leading Airman W. J. Clinton, were already in their cockpits when he arrived. The single engine was already warming up when a runner panted up with a message from the control room.

"It's Dover, sir. They say the enemy's speed is now estimated at 27 knots."

This was important; the Swordfish would aim their torpedoes to allow for the estimated speed of the targets. The runner was sent to pass this information to each pilot in turn.

Esmonde gave another quick look upwards for signs of the first arrivals from Biggin Hill and Hornchurch, saw there was nothing in sight and taxied down to the dip at the eastern end of the field and turned westwards into the wind. The engine roared for a few seconds, then, with a wave of his arm to the squadron behind, he sent the aircraft surging forward.

The time was 12.25 pm.

Gleave walked out on to the field to wave a salute to each plane as it roared off after the leader. He stood alone in the middle of the vast airfield watching the squadron form up behind their leader, two directly astern of him and the other coming up in the rear in Vic formation. He had watched the struggle within Esmonde when the news had come into the control room. Now he paid silent tribute to them all.

Esmonde led the squadron westwards at first away from Manston. Then he turned to fly back over the airfield. Until then the weather had been more amiable than over the Channel. Now a huge black cumulus cloud formed up directly overhead, hanging like some gigantic chandelier. The Swordfish, flying in line with the Vic astern, flew beneath it, turning black in its shadow.

To the solitary Gleave below, not easily given to romanticism or swayed by superstition, they took on the appearance of black phantom planes from an earlier war returning at this critical turning point in naval history to fight one more battle for England — as the "White Host on Horseback" had stiffened the British lines at Mons, and Drake's Drum had sounded at Trafalgar.

Gleave forced his eyes away, shook slightly and wondered vaguely at the sudden chill breeze which struck through his greatcoat as he hurried back to the station office. He was still gripped in the well of emotion at seeing for the first time a man who had become a friend cold-bloodedly decide to sacrifice his life when another course was open to him. It was calculated suicide.[11]

Seventeen young men flew with "Winkle" Esmonde. Each one took off that day with the same haunting fear in his face. The racking burden of decision had not been theirs to carry, but once their leader had given his orders, they obeyed and would follow him even to the point of no return.

He led them eastwards, flying like the birds at Drominagh — nose thrust eagerly into the wind.

---

[11] In telling me of this, Tom Gleave, now Group Captain, said: "Some sneer at fear — because they have never known real fear. Some sneer at emotion, too. I am not ashamed of it. Those Swordfish crews were courage personified — to me courage in the face of the worst of all fears is the supreme kind."

CHAPTER 9: THE DEVOTED ATTACK

At 1500 feet, and slightly to seawards of Manston, 825 Squadron orbited slowly, waiting for the arrival of their fighter escorts. In the front cockpit of *W-5984*, Esmonde glanced casually at the helmeted heads of the officers and sailors manning the Swordfish: he was grateful that, knowing the risks and the slim chances of survival, not one had failed to follow him. Whatever chances there were would depend almost entirely on fighters and luck — a large amount of luck.

Brian Rose in *W-5983* was almost caressing his tail; behind him and slightly above was *W-5907*, piloted by carefree, the world-is-mine-to-take-or-leave Colin Kingsmill, a sub-lieutenant in the Volunteer Reserve, Sub-Lieutenant R. M. Samples as Observer, and Leading Airman D. A. Bunce swivelling his guns; lower and further away was *W-4523* with the handsome sub-flight leader, Lieutenant Thompson, piloting, with Sub-Lieutenant Parkinson as Observer and Leading Airman E. Topping at the guns; next came *W-5985* with Sub-Lieutenants Wood and Fuller-Wright and Leading Airman Wheeler; Sub-Lieutenants Peter Bligh and Bill Beynon with Leading Airman Smith brought up the rear in *W-5978*.

Six aircraft, six torpedoes and eighteen men; out at sea were two battle cruisers, a heavy cruiser, six large destroyers, 34 E-boats and an assortment of flak ships — and, of course, the Luftwaffe. Esmonde glanced again at his watch. It was now 12.29, four minutes after rendezvous time.

The weather was deteriorating; according to reports at Manston it would be closing in near the Belgian coast. The enemy battle fleet was drawing away with every minute and the squadron knew their leader must be thinking of his former resolve never again to take a Swordfish to attack a retreating enemy.

Esmonde was primarily concerned about the fighter escort. To set off without cover would place the squadron at the mercy of the Luftwaffe; they might be destroyed before the enemy was reached. If by some miraculous fortune their cumbersome aircraft, dragged back to about 85 knots by the weight of armed torpedoes, should stagger to within range, they would face the massed fire of the fleet.

He took the squadron to the coast and continued orbiting over Ramsgate. Suddenly a quick smile and a wave of his hand indicated ten fighters streaking towards and above them. At last some escorts were coming. It was 12.32 pm.

Two more minutes passed; the smile had gone. No more fighters were in sight. He waved a hand for the formation to take station astern and led the way down to 50 feet and out to sea. Fifteen minutes and 23 miles separated him from the enemy. Suicide it might be, but if lives were not to be lost in vain there was no more time to lose. The eighteen men wiped all thoughts from their minds except the important object of delivering a decisive blow.

Although an easily manoeuvrable aircraft even when "bombed up", there was not much room for aerobatics at 50 feet. With the pathetically scanty escort of ten Spitfires, each of the six naval pilots recognised one unalterable fact: he would have to fly as never before once the Luftwaffe pounced.

Escorting the slow torpedo bombers was no easy task for the Spitfires. To maintain the mere semblance of an escort they were forced to weave widely, soar and swoop, at minimum throttle to stay in the vicinity.

Ten miles east of Ramsgate, in thickening overcast and with visibility not more than four miles, the meagre force made contact with the enemy. Two flights of Me109s swooped in below the Spitfires and ran down the sides of the Swordfish formation firing as each aircraft came into their sights. Machine-gun bullets and cannon shells whipped through the fabric of the fuselages.

But this skirmish caused little undue worry. The handful of Biggin Hill fighters broke up the enemy and chased them northwards. At once the weakness of the escort became apparent. Another flight of enemy fighters had been lurking above waiting for this opportunity. They poured down on the Swordfish in a chattering rain, driving through the formation between the two flights.

However, it was not yet serious. Experience had shown that the Swordfish could out-manoeuvre the Me109 with comparative ease, and by constant weaving and dodging they were able to leave the Luftwaffe with plenty of empty air to shoot at. The Spitfires came racing back before the next attack and the torpedo bombers were able to re-form.

Esmonde's flight was in line astern about 50 yards apart. Thompson's sub-flight followed half a mile behind still in Vic formation — unusual in view of Esmonde's instructions for both flights to maintain station in line astern.

Twenty Me109s gathered for a massed dive to port, but three Spitfires rushed across and broke up the attack before it really started. About half a dozen got through and converged on Esmonde and Brian Rose, who banked in opposite directions with wingtips nearly touching the water, while their gunners sprayed the attackers. Another reverse weave and the two aircraft re-formed.

This constant twisting away from the enemy was reducing speed over the ground to a dangerous extent, probably not more than 50 knots. With the enemy making a good 30 knots it would take time to overhaul the fleet, and each pilot was acutely conscious of his fuel position. It was Esmonde's hated chase of an enemy racing away from him.

Long trailers of ripped fabric streamed from the aircraft — a frightening sight without any real danger. For these aircraft could absorb tremendous punishment in the body. Their fabric fuselages offered no resistance to impact shells. Most exposed parts were the engines, fuel tanks and the crews themselves.

At 12.50 they sighted the battle fleet, and for the first time the full strength of the enemy lay before their eyes with sickening reality. Ahead and stretching into the mists on either side were the long lines of escorts forming the outer and inner screens. Past these was the close destroyer screen hugging the sides of the great battle cruisers swathed in the fumes and smoke of their own broadsides, then being fired at the retreating MTBs.

To airmen, the sky above presented an even worse picture. At 500-feet levels ranging from 50 to 2000 feet and covering the entire visible sky swarmed hundreds of Luftwaffe fighters — the most immense air "umbrella" ever seen covering a force at sea. The eighteen youngsters making a heavy, ungainly passage almost at sea level into this floating, flying turmoil recoiled involuntarily at the sight, and more than one Swordfish swerved wildly as pilots obeyed natural impulses to run.

The leader's plane maintained its even course, nose pointing directly at the first ship in the battle formation, *Scharnhorst*. Discipline overcame the shock to his crews and nervously guided aircraft re-formed behind him. If any doubt of what they might face had been present before, it was swamped now by the certain knowledge that in a very few minutes they must die.

At this moment more than any other, the power of leadership in Eugene Esmonde was demonstrated as being dominant over the fear of death. Apart from those few frightening, faltering seconds, pilots, observers and gunners flew steadily onwards as the first fiery wall of tracers swept up from the E-boats, the first fused shell broadsides burst in their faces and a hundred fighters broke away from the "umbrella" to crush the threatening scorpion at the battle fleet's side.

The ten Spitfires which had accompanied them from the coast were lost in a maze of dogfights, while a vast air battle spread up from the south, where the remainder of the Biggin Hill Wing were climbing into the rear of the "umbrella". Arriving at the rendezvous late, these fighter squadrons had headed out to sea, in the hope of catching up with the Swordfish. They were too far to the south, however, and turned north to meet the first of the Luftwaffe's rearguard just as the battle squadron engaged the Swordfish. Indirectly, and with only slight effect against such overwhelming numbers, they were contributing to the best of their ability to the safety of the of the torpedo bombers.

The Hornchurch wing, also missing the rendezvous, proceeded to Calais, where there was no sign of the enemy, so the squadron maintained a short patrol before returning to base.

Esmonde drove his aircraft through the first flak barrage and over the outer screen. The second barrage of heavier flak fire from the destroyers and the main battle formation converged on him, while the fighters swooped down on the tails of the rear aircraft in waves of three at a time — one coming in from astern and the others from each side.

Brian Rose followed his leader across the outer screen with Kingsmill, harried by fighters, dropping gradually astern. The main Luftwaffe swarm gathered for the kill round the Vic formation of Thompson's sub-flight, still maintaining station half a mile astern.

Three thousand yards to go.

The light flack slackened as more fighters closed in around the leading flight. Esmonde began weaving again to shake the aim of fighters attacking on his tail. A new menace struck Brian Rose; FW190s, fast and more manoeuvrable than the Messerschmitts, and armed with cannon, concentrated their waves of attacks on his Swordfish.

His guns stopped their clamour and Edgar Lee glanced round to see Johnson slumped over the machine-guns. He stood up, turned and reached back, trying to lift the gunner's body clear of the guns. This proved impossible, but a sudden idea made him call into the intercom:

"I'll keep watch astern, Brian, and let you know when the bastards are coming."

In the middle of a suicidal battle, he stood upright staring into the noses of attacking FW190s; and at his urgent shouts of "*Now*, Brian, *now*..." the pilot swerved violently towards either beam attackers, causing them to climb on their tails to avoid collisions, while the stern attacker would invariably overshoot.

In this manner, and in a way which repudiates gallantry as an apt description, the young sub-lieutenant from Ipswich stood half in and half out of his cockpit to gaze at the enemy guns, forcing himself to guess the moment they would fire so that he could shout warnings to his pilot.

He could see in the third Swordfish of the sub-flight, behind and slightly below, Samples and Bunce brandishing their arms and shouting insults at the enemy, although their words were lost in the din.

Facing astern, he missed another incredible act of courage by Esmonde's gunner, Clinton. But Flight Lieutenant Michael Crombie, flying in a Spitfire overhead, nearly collided with an enemy fighter as he gazed down at the leading Swordfish, fascinated at the sight of the gunner out of his rear cockpit and sitting astraddle the body, beating with gloved hands at tiny flames licking from the fabric. It is likely that the fire was caused by tracer bullets passing through the fuselage and threatened either to engulf the gunner's cockpit or had blinded him when he most wanted to fire his guns. He had climbed out, extinguished the fire with his hands and then returned to his guns.

Esmonde was over the inner screen now, and wide holes in his fuselage showed where heavy shells had hit and passed on through. It was the turn of the main 11-inch armament of the battle cruisers to come into action. Belching smoke and flame they laid down a thick carpet barrage ahead of him, sending up a wall of water which crashed down on the limping Swordfish. No attempt was made to hit him. At almost nought feet even a slight fall of water would send him down into the sea. The next broadside hit the water fifty feet in front of Brian Rose, and the aircraft waggled wildly as the plumes of water cascaded down into the cockpits drenching the engine.

Edgar Lee turned on wobbly, nerveless legs to identify the targets just as the rear of Rose's cockpit blew to pieces in front of him. A cannon-shell had whipped through the aircraft, passed between his own body and the fuselage and exploded against the thin steel plating on the pilot's backrest. The full force of shrapnel and splinters plunged deep into Rose's back. Lee heard the pilot groan; the aircraft's nose dipped dangerously. He leaned forward, shouting hoarse urgent warnings to pull up.

The pilot's hunched body moved and the Swordfish came under control again. Breathing heavily with exertion, Lee looked ahead again, and to his astonishment they had cleared the inner screen. Over the engine cowling loomed the massive targets.

In front, close enough for Lee to see the crew, was Esmonde's Swordfish, and in that instant its lower port wing vanished, shot clean away by a shell designed to make a watersplash, but which ricocheted instead and hit *W-5984*. Lee saw the nose point down towards the water and the jerky movements in the front cockpit as Esmonde fought to bring the plane under control. Gradually the nose came up again and steadied.

It seemed to Lee that his leader was heading for the *Scharnhorst*, so he called out to Rose to alter course slightly to bring *Gneisenau* directly ahead. As they moved slowly across, a burst of tracer bullets whined past and tore into Esmonde's cockpit.

Fifteen hundred yards to go.

The flak barrage fell off again as more Luftwaffe fighters drove down on the Swordfish, which, miraculously, were not only still flying, but looked as if they might succeed in their attack.

Desperately wounded in the head and back, Esmonde held his course for *Scharnhorst*. In the cockpits behind him slumped the figures of Williams and the brave Clinton, both killed. With no defences, his guns silent, he had crossed two screens and dodged milling flights of enemy fighters.

The cost of duty was being paid; life was quickly draining from his body when he took a last look through a film of blood covering his eyes, pulled the aircraft's nose up into the wind for the last time and released the torpedo.

A dozen fighters fell upon his mortally crippled Swordfish, pumping bullets into his already lifeless body. Still standing in his cockpit, Lee watched his leader crash into the sea while the torpedo ran towards the target.

The entire scene flashed across his mind in seconds, then he was absorbed by the urgent need to keep shouting at Rose to prevent the pilot lapsing into unconsciousness. Somehow Rose kept the swimming blessedness of oblivion at bay and with nearly sightless eyes automatically obeyed his observer's instructions.

"Keep the nose up, Brian. For God's sake keep it up. Now a little to starboard. Christ, we've been hit."

A heavy thump in the nose startled Rose from his lethargy and put strength back into his arms as he hauled painfully at the controls. Leaning over his shoulder, Lee shouted:

"Look, the fuel gauge. It's falling down."

Rose nodded and Lee leant out over the side. The fuselage was streaming with petrol. A shell had exploded in the main tank. He touched Rose's head and gestured to the gauge and then over the side. The pilot's head jerked in acknowledgment and his fingers flipped over the switch to the emergency tank holding a reserve of fifteen gallons. The engine coughed, faltered and spluttered to life again; the Swordfish skimmed the water as it caught speed and pointed at *Gneisenau*.

A thousand yards to go.

"Now, Brian. Fire the torpedo."

Lee's urgent scream snapped the pilot alive, and with obvious effort he grasped the release lever, pulling it down.

The Swordfish leapt upwards with the loss of weight. Lee glanced down to see the torpedo bounce on the water and then run towards the target. His eyes flickered ahead, automatically registering that they had fired not at *Gneisenau*, but at *Prinz Eugen*.

A feeble voice reached Lee through the intercom:

"I think we might try making it to the outer screen. You shout directions."

Lee looked down at Rose's head, and just the faintest gleam of hope sparkled suddenly in his eyes. The incidental thought crossed his mind that Esmonde's torpedo must have missed. Certainly by now theirs should have hit. Another miss. He could see the white faces of the German gunners behind the sparking muzzles of their guns as the seemingly huge ship altered course towards the aircraft to evade the torpedo.

"Up, Brian. Up fast. We're going into him."

The nose jumped upwards and the Swordfish passed over the German cruiser — close. Sweat poured down Lee's face, drenching his eyes. They were in the middle of the battle formation now and it was on him that their chances rested for getting out.

The enemy fighters were leaving them alone; they were torpedoless and presented no further threat to the ships. To starboard Lee saw Kingsmill's Swordfish limping over the destroyer screen, taking tremendous punishment from the flak. Once inside, fighters pounced again.

The two top cylinders of the single engine were shot away, the engine itself burst into flames and the port wing caught fire. All three of the crew were severely wounded, but Kingsmill was fighting with what strength he had left to keep the Swordfish under control. At 2000 yards he released his torpedo at *Prinz Eugen* and turned away, heading down towards the stern of the battle fleet.

In his overwrought condition, Lee felt the joy of seeing at least one of his squadron retire. Kingsmill's engine went dead as he reached the wake of the last E-boat and the aircraft flopped, rather than crashed, into the sea. Each of the crew painfully clambered from their cockpits, and fell exhausted into the water. Their dinghy had been destroyed in the burning wing.

The E-boat continued on its course, but an MTB leaving the scene saw the aircraft land and raced over to rescue the survivors.

Meanwhile, Lieutenant Saunders in MTB *44*, had seen the plight of the Swordfish piloted by Brian Rose. It came erratically out over the inner screen with only ineffectual flak half-heartedly put up to stop it. Rose had summoned his waning strength again for the next emergency.

"I'll have to try and ditch her in a minute," he called out in his strongest voice since the attack.

Lee nodded and settled down in his cockpit in readiness for the bump. The Swordfish crossed the outer screen, coughed; Rose held the controls firmly. The aircraft lost height slowly and belly-landed perfectly in the rising sea.

Above them Thompson's sub-flight were weaving their way into the attack, still in Vic formation. The flak eased off while the fighters leapt in again. Three FW190s with undercarriages lowered and flaps fully down to reduce speed were on the tails of the Vic spewing cannon fire into each Swordfish in turn.

They crossed the outer screen, approached the inner, losing height. Struggling to fly, bodies in ribbons, wings like skeletons with the struts showing bare and crews who must not only be wounded but dead or dying, they crossed the line of destroyers and met the smoky spumes of water thrown up by the heavy ships' "water-spout" barrage.

For a brief instant the Luftwaffe drew off, and quite alone but still maintaining a steady course the three Swordfish vanished into the spray of the "water-spout". What happened behind the wall of that dreadful barrage remains a mystery. It is officially presumed that they dropped their torpedoes before the end. In this event it must also be assumed that they came out from that horrible cascade of cordite and water with the mask of death already set on their faces as they followed Eugene Esmonde into the Narrow Sea.

Neither the three Swordfish nor the nine youngsters who manned them were ever seen again.

W-5983 bobbed jerkily in the choppy sea. Brian Rose, only semi-conscious after the effort of crash landing, was slumped sideways in his cockpit. Edgar Lee ripped out the yellow rubber dinghy, pulled the toggle and lashed it to the side of the aircraft. When it looked as if it would float and had somehow escaped the torrent of bullets which had swept through the aircraft, he tried to pull the dead gunner, Johnson, from the rear cockpit. This proved difficult, so he climbed over the side and worked his way aft. The battle had left him weak and tired; try as he might, he could not lift the weight of the dead man. In the for'ard cockpit, Rose stirred, trying to extricate himself. Lee scrambled along to him and eventually managed to topple the pilot over the side of the cockpit into the dinghy.

In the same instant the stricken Swordfish began to roll on its side before going down. Lee jerked at the tie-rope, but it stuck. His frozen fingers worked frantically at the knot. He was frightened that, having come through so far, they would be dragged down by the sinking aircraft.

The knot came clear just in time. With a cracking of struts, the Swordfish folded in the middle and sank — a brave coffin for the courageous Johnson.

Rose was fully conscious now and moaning with pain. His left arm was useless, but he persisted in using his right to help Lee bail out the dinghy. The weather had become worse and it was difficult to see more than two or three miles. Above, hundreds of fighters were engaged in innumerable dogfights.

The tiny yellow dinghy rose on the crest of a wave and a stream of tracer bullets whished over the heads of the stranded airmen. Lee looked around in sudden alarm. Over to starboard a long line of E-boats which had been prowling astern of the main battle fleet were steaming past about a mile away, each boat taking his turn to concentrate light machine-gun fire at the bobbing target.

The observer pushed the pilot flat on the bottom of the dinghy and crouched over him. The bailing went on, as did their prayers when every few seconds a wave lifted them into the sights of the passing enemy.

While hugging the bottom of the dinghy, Lee searched its contents, finding a bundle of pyrotechnic distress flares and a tin of aluminium dust. When thrown over the sea, the dust formed a silver pool round the dinghy which could be seen from the air for miles. Excitedly, Lee opened the tin and tossed the contents overboard. Unfortunately he was too overwrought to even consider the direction from which the wind was blowing, and aimed to windward. The dust blew back in a cloud, covering both dinghy and its occupants in silver. The exposed sides of Lee and Rose glittered brilliantly.

After half an hour the enemy firing ceased, only to be replaced by another danger — the bitter wind and freezing water.

"It was decidedly unpleasant," Lee reported later. "I tried to keep Rose working at the bailing, but the cold was not only acting as an anaesthetic against pain, it was also making him very tired. Every time he dozed I had to punch him awake."

Another hour passed before Lee considered the position desperate enough to use his only remaining distress signals, the flares. He had been reluctant to use them, in case an E-boat steamed up, in which event they might be killed or taken prisoner.

He jerked hard at the tape on one of the flares, automatically lighting it. After a brief splutter nothing seemed to happen. Then he suddenly noticed he was pointing the flare directly at Rose's face. He lifted his arm and in the same instant red balls of fire shot into the air to hover and sink slowly back into the sea. The thought of so nearly hurting his pilot, perhaps fatally, made him momentarily sick.

More than an hour before, MTB *44* had begun searching for survivors. She was joined later by the boat which had picked up Kingsmill and his crew. Patiently, the two boats swept the area in decreasing circles until at 3 pm a lookout shouted:

"Flares ahead, sir."

Both boats increased speed until, in fading light and lowering visibility, they were able to sight the yellow dinghy. Rose and Lee saw the boats at the same time. Unaccountably they were convinced their rescuers were Germans and greeted the first hails in silence. The boats drew alongside, and Lee gazed up in astonishment at the sound of English voices. A slow smile creased his pinched face and he collapsed weakly to the floor of the dinghy. A sailor jumped overboard into the icy sea, tied the dinghy alongside the MTB and lifted each of the airmen up to willing hands. A few minutes later and Rose was wrapped in bed asleep, while Lee was swathed in towels sipping the one drink he detests — rum.

Before dusk the MTBs returned to Dover, where Rose and Lee were rushed to the "melting oven" — a crude invention designed to thaw out survivors or shot-down pilots. It was a circular shed in the docks in which bunks were placed down the middle. Overhead, rows of high-voltage electric lights blazed down on cold bodies. Lee testifies that it was one of the simplest and most efficient devices he met in the war. After a brief twenty minutes, he and Rose glowed with warmth; then they were separated, the pilot being taken to hospital and Lee to Dover Castle to report to Admiral Ramsay.

Edgar Lee, son of an Ipswich electrical engineer, was one of five who survived, and of those he was the only one who could stand on his feet. It is impossible to say he came through unscathed; for the scars on his mind are indelible. Thirteen of his comrades perished.

The results of this devoted attack, in which eighteen men protected by fabric challenged 4000 shielded by armour plate, could not be known at the time: the fact that they flew sufficed to fill a glorious chapter in the history of the Fleet Air Arm.

After hearing Lee's report, Admiral Ramsay signalled the Admiralty:

> *In my opinion the gallant sortie of these six Swordfish constitutes one of the finest exhibitions of self-sacrifice and devotion to duty that the war has yet witnessed.*

In the evening of that same day Lee was driven back to Manston, where, as senior surviving officer of the squadron, there was much he should do before being sent on leave.

He gathered the ground staff in the crew room and relived for them the events of the day, so that they should share his own pride in their commander. It was nearly midnight when they left him alone in the small hut where only a few hours earlier he had been deafened by the cheerful ribaldry of his friends.

He looked round the walls. Meticulously nailed above every peg was a name: beneath it were the clothes each officer and gunner would wear when he returned. He would have to parcel them up now — thirteen parcels of personal effects to be sent with thirteen letters of sympathy to nearest relatives. His face twisted savagely in sudden overwhelming grief. Reaction from prolonged strain was setting in.

After a last lingering look round the room, he turned and walked out.

The heights to which the human spirit may rise are unpredictable, and the effort of will, which is the weapon of the spirit, transcends failure or success. By the decision to fly that day Esmonde, Lee, Rose,[12] Kingsmill and the rest created an imperishable example.

Most of the squadron died following "Winkle" Esmonde; but he was, according to the Admiralty, "a wise and brave captain with too much integrity to waste either their lives or his own in an attack which held no hope of success". In this instance he flew because five squadrons of fighters would protect him — fighters which would reduce the mission to one of acceptable risk rather than calculated sacrifice.

Few felt the loss of Eugene Esmonde as deeply as Wing Commander Gleave. He had seen the squadron leave and suffered with Esmonde the agony of waiting for an escort

---

[12] With Lee, Brian Rose received the DSO. He was killed in a flying accident later in the war. The three other survivors were also decorated and posthumous awards were made to the thirteen who died.

which failed to appear. In the evening he made his welcome to Edgar Lee brief, for he was unwilling to intrude on the young officer's deep personal suffering.

Instead Gleave retired to his office and wrote what had been on his mind since late afternoon when first reports of the Swordfish massacre had reached Manston, and Lee had given his report. He addressed his letter to Air Vice-Marshal Leigh-Mallory for forwarding at his discretion to the proper naval authorities. In the formal stilted verbose prose beloved by the Service administration, he said:

> Concerning pilots and crews of 825 Squadron which operated from Manston against *Scharnhorst*, *Gneisenau* and *Prinz Eugen*, attached is the report of Sub-Lieutenant Lee. As Officer Commanding this station to which 825 Squadron was attached for operational purposes, and having been fully acquainted with their operational activities and the circumstances attendant thereto in respect of the above operation against enemy warships which resulted in the loss of the entire Squadron and seventy-five per cent of their crews. I respectfully submit that it would not be presumptuous on my part to express an opinion on the manner in which Lieutenant-Commander Esmonde and the crews under his command carried out their duties on this occasion.
>
> I discussed the operation with Lieutenant-Commander Esmonde prior to the squadron taking off at 12.30. His pilots and crews present at this meeting displayed signs of great enthusiasm and keenness for the job they were about to undertake and it was no doubt due to Lieutenant-Commander Esmonde's leadership that such a fine spirit prevailed.
>
> Nothing more was heard of the squadron until the five survivors were brought ashore.
>
> The German battleships were undoubtedly protected by a terrific barrage of flak and covered by one of the biggest

fighter screens ever seen. Against this, the determination and gallantry shown by Lieutenant-Commander Esmonde and his pilots and crews is beyond any normal praise.

I am of the opinion that Lieutenant-Commander Esmonde is well worthy of the posthumous award of the Victoria Cross.

It must have been the first — if not the only — occasion on record of an RAF officer recommending a naval officer not even serving under him for the Victoria Cross.

Admiralty records say of Esmonde:

"He was free to act as he thought best, and believed he might succeed. That he was taking tremendous risks he knew, but was prepared to face them, as he had faced other risks many times before."

No such sanguine acceptance of a brave death existed outside Whitehall.

At Dover a pall of resentful anger clouded the Command. Neither Admiral Ramsay nor his staff were prepared to treat the loss of 825 Squadron as an inevitable casualty of war. In a personal message to the Fleet Air Arm base at Lee-on-Solent the next day, the Admiral wrote:

I cannot help but regard the miscarriage of the plan to provide fighter escorts for the Swordfish as a major tragedy of this war.

Until the time they took off I had thought all arrangements were proceeding satisfactorily. Had I known that the fighter escorts might not keep their rendezvous I would have told Lieutenant-Commander Esmonde to remain on the ground: indeed I would have forbidden the flight as an order.

This was the first of many bitter recriminations which were to follow in the wake of the Channel dash. Coastal Command were desperately trying to mount an attack with widely-dispersed forces; Bomber Command were sending messages across the country recalling crews and frantically briefing as many aircraft as could be bombed up and sent off before the enemy escaped under cover of worsening weather and approaching darkness; Fighter Command were so deeply committed that few if any squadrons could be spared for the vital escort duties which "Fuller" had insisted were paramount; and at Harwich, six old destroyers were already racing across the North Sea to intercept.

Vice-Admiral Ciliax, in *Scharnhorst*, smiled grimly and muttered to his staff: "Those Swordfish did well to get their torpedoes away. The English are throwing their mothball navy at us now, apparently."

His official report of the subsequent MTB and Swordfish attacks is remarkable for its lack of any real sense of danger aboard the heavy ships.

> At 12.30 the battery Siegfried, west of Calais, returned the fire from the Dover guns, firing twelve rounds into the British port. It is hoped that they will be discouraged by this retaliation. At the same time we sight an enemy torpedo-boat and know that at least the enemy will be warned of our presence.
>
> The tension on board the German ships, which had arisen to its maximum because of the hours of waiting, is slackened by these events and can be worked off in the defence of continuous attacks by sea and air which are now beginning.
>
> The 4th E-boat Flotilla to port which had laid a smoke screen previously is attacked first by two Spitfires and then by 5-6 MTBs. The flotilla drives the English boats away from the formation and the destroyers *Friedrich Ihn* and *Hermann Schoemann* move into action, scattering the torpedo-boat

formation and pursue it to the Goodwin Sands so that it cannot succeed in making an attack on the ships.

The 5th Torpedo Boat Flotilla joins up from Flushing and the Admiral Commanding Battleships has now assembled all the escort forces around the formation.

According to reports from the leader of the Luftwaffe formations overhead, the first air wave is arriving and consists of eight torpedo-carrying planes with eighteen to twenty Spitfires. Under pressure of the German fighters, the torpedoes are released from a great distance, seemingly without target. The Luftwaffe is responsible for shooting down three aircraft, the *Scharnhorst* for one and *Prinz Eugen* for three of the four bombers which directly attacked the ships.

This first attacking wave had just grown less violent when the formation entered the dangerously mined area — the one in which the destroyer *Bruno Heinemann* had been sunk — and it would hardly have been possible to avoid torpedoes because of the sands to port and mines to starboard.

This last sentence carries with it the German Admiral's greatest worry. Once through this narrow passage, he would have room to manoeuvre when under attack. For the moment he had to reduce speed. It was the critical moment for the Coastal Command torpedo bombers to launch their attack.

As the battle squadron slowed down, anxious eyes peered into the mist, searching the horizon and scanning the overcast sky. Desperately needed minutes passed. Nothing happened. If it were not for the innumerable dog-fights heard overhead, it would appear that Britain was according Ciliax free passage.

He passed through the dangerous funnel into wider waters, and at 2 pm ordered the fleet to resume the dash at full speed. His principal concern now was to keep within the limits of the swept channel. The squadron was relying upon the marker boats anchored on each side for navigational safety. But these could be seen only with difficulty at two miles, sometimes less than half a mile. They emitted direction-finding signals on their wireless to "home" the fleet — a procedure which merely lessened Ciliax's headache without removing it.

Still there was no sign of attack. There were those in the German crews who began to suspect that the operation might succeed. Their optimism was to be rudely shaken.

At 2.30 pm — when Coastal and Bomber Commands in massed assault might have saved the day but instead were frantically endeavouring to bring organised confusion out of disorganised chaos — *Scharnhorst* reeled under the impact of a tremendous explosion. Her throbbing engines were silent and she came to a wallowing standstill. The mine had damaged her propeller shafts. In Ciliax's opinion there was little likelihood that she could be repaired before the main air attacks developed. He decided to continue in command of the dash by transferring with his staff to the destroyer *Z-29*, which was ordered alongside.

It was a daring decision made possible only because the RAF and the Royal Navy were so conspicuously absent. The destroyer closed the stricken *Scharnhorst* in the choppy sea, bumped hard against her on the rising crest of a wave. In that brief second when she lay poised on a level with the battle cruiser's welldeck, Ciliax and his staff leapt across the gap to stumble safely on the destroyer's foredeck.

With propellers churning astern, *Z-29*, now the headquarters ship, turned northwards and headed after the main fleet at full speed. For a moment Ciliax stared hard at his flagship, vaguely wondering if, having come so far, she would survive the ordeal that must lie ahead — it might be the beginning of the end.

CHAPTER 10: SALVAGE OF A SACRIFICE

The MTB and Swordfish attacks had died away a few minutes after 1 pm. There was an imperative need now for the assault against the enemy to be sustained throughout the remaining hours of daylight. Of the three Royal Air Force Commands, only the available fighters had been committed to action. Coastal Command were the most conveniently situated for the next phase of the battle.

A formidable responsibility fell upon the Command. The enemy had been at sea for more than fifteen hours; he had run the Dover gauntlet untouched; he was now approaching the Dutch coast on the last leg of his dash. Confusion ruled out an immediate Bomber Command offensive and, unless the ships were severely crippled in the meantime, there was every chance that the bombers would prove ineffective.

Nearest to the enemy were the seven Beaufort torpedo bombers of 217 Squadron based at Thorney Island (Portsmouth). At 11.55 am the staff officer controlling operations of this detachment rang through to Hornchurch with a request that No11 Group provide fighter cover to rendezvous with the Beauforts over Manston about 1.30 pm. The Hornchurch controller was quite naturally caustic in his reminder to Thorney Island that a request of this sort was looking a bit too far ahead of events — the battle had not yet begun. His fighters were quite likely to be required earlier by more speedily mounted attacks. However, if Thorney Island could guarantee to have their aircraft over Manston at 1.30 he would see what could be done.

This satisfied the Beaufort station, and preparations were made for takeoff which soon revealed a brace of most unfortunate errors. Two of the Beauforts were armed with bombs instead of torpedoes and a third aircraft developed a technical fault which eluded all attempts by the ground staff to trace it. As the transfer of bombs to torpedoes would take considerable time, it was decided that these three aircraft should follow when ready.

The four serviceable Beauforts were properly armed for a torpedo attack and ready for takeoff. Crews were called to the briefing room and told to fly to Manston, where fighter escorts would lead them to their target. Not a word was whispered about the nature of the target or the vital importance of the mission.

The break-up of the squadron delayed the departure of the four Beauforts led by Pilot Officer Carson to the extent that they took off at 1.25 pm, only five minutes before they were due to meet the fighters over Manston.

The fighter cover kept the rendezvous on time and circled above the airfield for more than five minutes. Disgusted at this waste of effort, Wing Commander Gleave telephoned Hornchurch to ask bluntly: "What the devil are your fighter chaps doing circling over here for so long?" When he informed No11 Group that the Beauforts had not arrived, the fighters were at once ordered to proceed independently to the target area. This order was first telephoned to 16 Group headquarters at Thorney Island and immediately approved.

"That's all right. You send your chaps ahead and tell them to look out for the Beauforts when they arrive."

It was agreed that this information with the orders to proceed independently should be passed to the two forces — by R/T to the Spitfires and W/T to the Beauforts.[13]

Unfortunately, No 16 Group forgot that their Beauforts had recently exchanged W/T for R/T, with the result that the Beaufort squadron did not receive the message.

Pilot Officer Carson led the four aircraft over Manston twenty minutes late and, having received no orders, proceeded to circle the airfield waiting for someone to tell him what was going on. After some minutes of this Carson and his pilots, not realising that their own escort had been and gone, began wondering why the many fighters also orbiting before setting off on other duties would have nothing to do with them.

Fifteen minutes passed before Carson decided to head out to sea in the direction in which other aircraft seemed to be travelling back and forth. With his wing man keeping immaculate station he branched out of the orbit and headed for France.

Alas, the two rear Beauforts had been forced to drop back to allow other aircraft through the orbit, and were half a circle away, facing the opposite direction, when Carson and his companion set off. They banked round, saw no sign of their leader, so continued orbiting, on the assumption that if Carson was momentarily lost he would not be pleased to return to the circuit and find them missing.

Another reason was the arrival in the orbit of a likely looking flock of Hudson light bombers who looked well prepared for business. The Beauforts moved round the circle up to their tails and stayed there.

On the ground mild chuckles at the Beauforts' behaviour soon gave way to anger as their circling persisted.

"What the hell do they think they're up to?" muttered the controller angrily. "Playing ring-a'-ring-a'-roses or something?"

---

[13] R/T — Radio Telephone; W/T — Ordinary Wireless communication.

All attempts failed to contact the pair on W/T, with which they were supposed to be equipped.

Eventually the pilot of one Beaufort beckoned to the other in a downward direction. The fuel position was becoming critical, and in any event he was bored. They landed at 2.45 pm — an hour and fifteen minutes after the arranged rendezvous with the fighters.

The two pilots strolled into the control room and asked: "What's going on? No one seems to be taking any notice of us at all. What's all the flap about, anyway?"

"You've been briefed. Suppose you tell us what you were doing up there for the last forty minutes," the controller snapped back.

"Well, sir, we were simply told to rendezvous with some fighters over here and follow them to our target. We don't quite know what the target is yet, sir."

The pilot made this admission with obvious embarrassment. The controller gaped in astonishment.

"You mean to say that no one has told you what you are here for?"

"No, sir."

No further time was wasted. The two pilots were briefed, their aircraft refuelled and they took off for the Belgian coast — they were now an hour and a half late.

The enemy would prove hard to find. Thick overcast from which black wisps of cloud hung down into the smokescreens and gunsmoke provided effective protection against sea and air attacks. It was enough to make one pilot write into his official report:

> In the short hours which elapsed between the moment when the presence of the enemy ships was signalled and when the striking force arrived to attack it, the enemy vanished into a

protecting curtain of mist. To fight such an enemy is often to fight a shadow and recalled to mind...

As the Fleet Air arm pilots had found earlier, the Beauforts ran into fighter trouble when still far from the enemy ships. But their speed, manoeuvrability and fire-power made them thorny meat for the Luftwaffe.

Dodging, twisting and searching, the two torpedo bombers cruised across the North Sea, now and then seeing what looked like a black shape but on closer examination proved to be thick cloud. Around them a confusion of FW190s, ME109s, Spitfires and Hurricanes sped about the sky, only the odd passer-by taking much notice of the Beauforts. This was enough to make both pilots peer even harder — they must be close; for the Luftwaffe would hardly ignore them unless they were already inside the flak area. Their guessing ended when the enemy suddenly revealed himself with a triple stream of tracer bullets which rocketed between the two aircraft.

Unhesitatingly, Pilot Officer Aldridge in the lead put his Beaufort into a steep dive down the line of tracers. It was his one opportunity to make contact with the enemy and he had no intention of missing it. Behind and to port, Pilot Officer Stewart followed his leader down, wobbling slightly as an accurately placed heavy flak barrage exploded just ahead, spewing cordite across his windscreen.

He was still trying to clear it when Aldridge flattened out and waggled his wingtips — the signal that he had sighted the ships. Stewart cleared his windscreen sufficiently to see the dark blur of a line of ships passing below led by a shape which resembled the *Prinz Eugen*. A mile to port of her he clearly saw the destroyers laying a smokescreen. Then his attention was gripped as the aircraft bucked and heaved under the impact of dense, heavy flak bursting beneath it.

Aldridge made a wide turn over the ships and out to the port side, losing height in readiness for the approach run. At visibility distance he turned inwards to be met with another fierce flak barrage which forced the Beauforts to bank away.

Their next attempt came from ahead of the ships and slightly to starboard. Once again the barrage spoiled the attack. The third try was a repeat from the port beam, and this time Stewart fought to within 2000 yards of *Prinz Eugen* and pressed the button to release his torpedo. Nothing happened. He pushed the button frantically, but the release gear had been damaged by the enemy's fire. He broke away, lost his leader and hurried out over the destroyer screen. After three miles he turned to try again in the desperate hope that if he tried long enough the torpedo might eventually come free.

Stewart's report later said:

"At that moment I saw two Me109s flying across in front of me. They circled and tried to get on our tail and the *Prinz Eugen* came into my sights. I pressed the tit and luckily the torpedo dropped while I was immediately involved in a fight with the Messerschmitts.

"The fight took us over to starboard towards the Dutch coast. My gunner shot one down and the other one made off. Only then did we discover that the aircraft had been hit by cannon twelve times.

"This action was fought near Over Flaker Island, off the Dutch coast. We thought the name highly appropriate.

"I think the cruiser altered course to avoid the torpedo, as my aim had been fairly accurate. At the point of firing I had a good view of her whole length as she stopped firing when the Messerschmitts crossed in front of me.

"There was no time to watch the torpedo run, as the party had started and I heard the rear gunner firing like mad. I tried to climb up towards the clouds, but they were too high for me to reach in time. So I went low over the sea.

"We were going flat out, and I jinked the Beaufort up and down and zigzagged all over the place. I could see tracers flying past the cockpit. Then I heard the rear gunner shout that he had got one of the Messerschmitts. It went down into the sea in a spiral dive with lots of smoke pouring from it.

"With only 20 feet to fall, I don't see how the German pilot could have pulled out in time to save himself. The other Me kept on coming until the rear gunner got a good long burst into him. The tracers stopped coming past the cockpit. That Me had gone home."

Another torpedo attack had failed. It was made at 3.45, exactly three hours after Esmonde had flown over the outer screen, four hours since the Command had been ordered to attack. During this intervening period in our assault Vice-Admiral Ciliax had passed through the narrow danger area, in which his manoeuvrability had been reduced and the chances of torpedo hits consequently increased. And *Scharnhorst* had been given the vital time she needed to repair her damage.

Meanwhile, the three Beauforts of 217 Squadron which had been left behind at Thorney Island arrived punctually over Manston to meet their fighter escorts. Once again none of the pilots knew the nature of the target or its whereabouts. Fortunately, the leader landed and received instructions to proceed against the battle fleet with top-cover escort only.

By now the enemy had moved outside radar range, but the Beauforts were also equipped with air-sea radar, and when in the target area they picked up the ships.

The enemy reacted immediately. Blinded by flak and roughly handled by fighters, the torpedo bombers pressed home their attack in foul-weather conditions.

The first Beaufort broke cloud right above the German battle squadron and was immediately covered in a flak barrage. To get clear of this he took a wide turn over the Dutch coast, where coastal flak surrounded his aircraft. Thoroughly incensed by these omens of a personal feud between himself and the Germans, he returned to the target area to carry out his attack. Once more the flak from the escorting screens and the heavy ships tore into his plane, wounding the crew and holing every part of the aircraft without damaging the controls. Unfortunately the torpedo release gear had been shot away and he was forced to abandon his attempt and return to Manston.

Coming over the English coast near Ramsgate, the coastal anti-aircraft batteries mistook him for a Heinkel and he was shot up for a fourth time. At Manston astonished ground crews and pilots crowded round his plane. There was no reason at all why it should have flown long enough to return from Holland.

The second of this trio was so badly damaged by fighters he was unable to drop his torpedo and eventually decided to return to Manston. As the aircraft approached the airfield the pilot was shocked to discover that his undercarriage had jammed up... and beneath the belly was an armed torpedo. He circled the airfield, desperately trying to release the undercarriage, which stubbornly refused to move. The fuel-gauge showed the tanks to be nearly empty. He decided to risk a belly landing on the most deserted part of the field.

Over the intercom, he called:

"I'm going to try and make it as soft as possible, but if that damn torpedo goes up it will be sudden death anyway."

The propellers whined into a higher pitch, the aircraft's nose dipped and the crew tensed for the impact. A few seconds later the Beaufort hit the grass field, the torpedo was wrenched from its grips to bounce clear of the aircraft, which skidded to a stop 100 yards away. Cut, bruised, with hands and legs trembling under the strain of the last few seconds, the crew climbed out to wave weakly at the rescuers heading in their direction in a lorry. The torpedo lay embedded in the earth, harmless now.

The third pilot, Sergeant Rowt, was making his first operational flight. He dropped his torpedo successfully while flying low through a flak barrage. When he came out to head for home, FW190s pounced on his tail spraying the Beaufort with long machine-gun bursts. His wireless operator and gunner were seriously wounded and the windscreen perspex shattered, a piece of it lodging in his right eye.

Then a fire broke out in the flare-chute, menacing the safety of the aircraft. Despite their wounds, the crew painfully fought the fire and eventually put it out. The aircraft returned safely.

The two Beauforts which had been led away towards France by Carson earlier in the afternoon found nothing exciting off the French coast — which is hardly surprising, as they were searching 50 miles to the south-west of the enemy — and headed back to Manston. Carson cannot be blamed for his detour, because he was still entirely ignorant of what his target was supposed to be.

The aircraft landed back at Manston at 3.35 pm and Carson reported to Gleave in the control room. After explaining what had happened, he was given the enemy's latest position.

His companion Beaufort was refuelling, so he took off alone. It was a plucky attack of which Coastal Command could well be proud. Prowling enemy fighter flights, deliberately avoiding combat with our fighters and lying in wait for torpedo carriers or bombers, plagued his passage across the North Sea to the Dutch coast.

The rear-gunner's firing went on almost continuously; flak poured past his cockpit as he weaved about, low ducks to the sea followed by steep climbs. Occasionally a Spitfire or Hurricane would swoop down to relieve the pressure on his tail.

The visibility held at three miles, but it was raining when he reached the target area and switched on his radar. At 4.40 pm he found the battle fleet and skimmed along the surface ahead of the leading E-boat of the outer screen. Light and heavy flak swirled in mad confusion, but his eyes were fixed on the broad hulk of the ship ahead — *Gneisenau*. He maintained steady course across the screen, then lifted the Beaufort up a little to cross the destroyers, one of which was frantically laying smoke down *Gneisenau*'s side. At 2000 yards he let go his torpedo and a heavy thumping noise came from the tail.

Two fighters were pumping cannon into the aircraft. He was only 30 feet above the sea, so a pull on the stick sent the aircraft heading for the clouds, tracer bullets colourfully accompanying his flight for safety.

The friendly clouds embraced him and he turned to head back for Manston, not knowing that *Gneisenau* had altered course to let his torpedo pass 20 yards down her side.

It had been a gallant single-handed attempt which came near to success. Pressed home in the face of determined flak and constant fighter interference, Carson's attack might have come closer to success had it been made two hours earlier, when

Gneisenau would have been in the narrow channel feared by Admiral Ciliax and unable to take the violent avoiding action she had done without fear of running aground or into a minefield.

Carson's return marked the end of the attempts by 217 Squadron, Coastal Command.

Vice-Admiral Ciliax had brought his fleet into the operation control area of the Home Command. Instead of being thankful for the protection of worsening weather, he alleged that it allowed the RAF to penetrate close without being seen.

It is understandable that the anxiety of the German gunners was increased when they had to open fire suddenly on aircraft which appeared from cloud and mist so close. But Ciliax takes no account of the difficulties which the pilots and crews were having in not only finding him, but in staying in the air at all. In the grey dullness and poor visibility of the entire battlefield it was an enormous strain on pilots to distinguish the surface of the sea. It was particularly arduous for the torpedo bombers, who had to fly low to drop their loads. More than one pilot found himself at the last minute flying directly into the sea.

Coastal Command's next attack was mounted by the fourteen Beauforts of No42 Squadron from Leuchars, on the east Scottish coast. Four days before, when he had issued his appreciation, Sir Philip Joubert had ordered them south to North Coates, a Coastal Command base near Hull. Heavy snowfalls had prevented the execution of these orders until the morning of the 12th.

That morning three of the aircraft were without torpedoes at takeoff but spare torpedoes awaited their arrival at North Coates. While en route southwards the squadron was informed that North Coates was snowbound and instructed to proceed to another Coastal Command airfield, Bircham Newton. Before their arrival a second warning that this airfield was also snowbound was received and the squadron diverted to Coltishall, a fighter airfield in East Anglia.

The squadron landed at 11.45 am, just as the news that the enemy was making his Channel dash flashed through the Command. Coltishall catered only for fighters, and the nearest torpedoes for the three unarmed Beauforts were at North Coates, which possessed a Mobile Torpedo Servicing Unit. This was ordered to Coltishall and arrangements made with local police authorities for the roads to be cleared and an escort to drive ahead of the lorries.

Unfortunately, the Mobile Torpedo Servicing Unit had not been called upon for several years and at once belied its name, showing evidence of rusty organisation. It was slow in getting started, loaded unnecessary equipment and instead of rushing the necessary torpedoes and compressed air in one or two lorries, it set out from North Coates in a long solemn column as though embarking on a safari. To be kind, the roads were also icy and the "Immobile Unit" — as it was known forever after — arrived at Coltishall roughly about the same time as the German battle fleet reached home waters.

More ill-luck struck No42 when on landing it was found that two of the aircraft could not take off again. The remaining nine aircraft left for Manston.

Their instructions were to link up with fighters, which would provide top cover during the trip to Holland, and some Hudson light bombers intended to provide diversionary bombing of the flak screens, and to follow them out to sea.

When the nine Beauforts arrived over Manston at 2.53 — three minutes late — eleven Hudson bombers were already orbiting at a low level and droves of fighters, waiting impatiently to land for re-fuelling and re-arming, circled above them. The Beauforts promptly tried to join the circuit on the tails of the Hudsons; but on the first attempt the Hudsons broke circuit, turned tightly and formed up on the tails of the Beauforts. The Beaufort commander was determined to carry out orders, so he led his aircraft out of the circuit and reformed behind the Hudsons. Once again the Hudson force turned and insisted upon circling behind the Beauforts.

This obstinate persistence of the Hudsons in attempting to follow the Beauforts which in turn were equally insistent upon following the Hudsons continued for more than half an hour, while below, Wing Commander Gleave and his staff watched this repeat of the earlier performance in angry amazement.

All efforts failed to attract the attention of the Beauforts and Hudsons. They had been told to expect escort all the way to the target, the fighters being instructed to supply only general cover in the Straits area. The fighters the Beaufort and Hudson pilots saw above them merely added to their confusion.

Thus, the whole formation of bombers and torpedo carriers orbited round the airfield, each taking turn to follow-my-leader in the most ridiculous manner, which would have been laughable had it not been vitally important for an attack to be made on the crippled *Scharnhorst* lying impotent in the North Sea.

Eventually, at 3.35 pm the Beaufort squadron leader tired of the game and, thoroughly exasperated, led his formation out of the orbit and headed for the position of the enemy he had been given at Coltishall — nearly an hour before. His own squadron formed up behind him and, one by one as they noticed his move, the Hudsons broke away to follow, until there were six hugging the tails of the rear Beauforts. But five

Hudsons stayed in circuit unaware of the departure of their friends. They continued orbiting for another half an hour until at 4 pm they at last withdrew from the circuit and set off for their home base at Bircham Newton.

At this point it should be made absolutely clear that the pilots of all these forces were each carrying out to the best of their ability the orders given them on the ground. They cannot be blamed for confusion caused by dislocated staff work.

The Beaufort squadron broke away only when it was obvious to the commander that something was so clearly wrong that he was justified in disobeying orders by heading out to the target.

His squadron accompanied by the six Hudsons made their way across the sea in thick cloud and light rain. The two formations quickly lost touch. The Hudsons investigated a radar contact, came down low beneath the cloud and sighted part of the enemy fleet to starboard. They attacked through fierce flak barrages and dropped their bombs on the outer screen. Two were shot down.

By this time six of the Beauforts had also made contact and released their torpedoes against *Gneisenau*. The other three had become lost in the mist. They did, however, sight the shapes of what appeared to be three big ships. The aircraft swooped down low and released their torpedoes, all three pilots later reporting their surprise that none of the ships fired a shot at them. They were to be even more surprised when reports of the battle indicated precisely what their targets had been.

This completed the operations of No42 Squadron.

At 12.20 pm — nearly an hour after the enemy had first been reported in the Channel by Victor Beamish — the fifteen Beauforts at St Evall, Cornwall, were ordered to Thorney Island. Cf these aircraft, three were already out on patrol over the Bay of Biscay. The remaining twelve arrived at Portsmouth at 2.30, where they were immediately ordered to "bomb up" prior to leaving for Coltishall to rendezvous with a fighter escort.

At 5 pm the Beauforts arrived over Coltishall to find no sign of the fighters. They circled for a few minutes before their commander eventually decided to set off without escort. At 5.41 he reached the last position of the enemy reported to him at Thorney Island. The enemy were by that time 40 miles to the north, dusk was giving way to night and visibility down to the extent that there was little hope of finding them. While searching low over the water, the squadron ran across four minesweepers, which put up a heavy concentration of light flak. The aircraft banked away and headed for home. Two of these aircraft failed to return, and it is most likely that in the darkness and mist they were unable to distinguish sky from sea and flew into the water.

The return of this squadron to Coltishall marked the end of Coastal Command's role in the Channel dash operations. It had been an unsuccessful role primarily because of delays caused by confusion over England. But once the enemy had been engaged, pilots and crews pressed home their attacks in the face of extremely fierce opposition with the determination and gallantry which characterised every action of the fighting men of both the Navy and RAF on February 12th, 1942.

By now the great German armada, strung out through breakdowns, manoeuvring to avoid torpedoes and through escorts constantly losing contact with the main fleet in the bad weather, was steaming past Amsterdam. In *Scharnhorst*, some 20 miles astern, engineers were hurriedly repairing the mine damage. So far her stopped hulk had evaded detection.

In all, fifteen Coastal Command aircraft attacked, two of these failing to drop their torpedoes. Two aircraft and six men were lost.

There was still time to salvage victory with the inspiration of Eugene Esmonde's sacrifice. The Harwich destroyers would attack next.

CHAPTER 11: THE SHIP THAT WOULDN'T DIE

To: HMS Campbell

From: V-A Dover.
Enemy battle cruisers passing Boulogne speed about 20 knots. Proceed
in execution of previous orders.

This signal from Vice-Admiral Ramsay at Dover to Captain C. T. M. Pizey, DSO, Commander of the 21st Destroyer Flotilla based at Harwich, sent the destroyer force held in readiness under "Fuller" into battle against the enemy fleet. Captain Pizey's nominal flotilla consisted at that time of his own ship, *Campbell*, and *Vivacious*. Also under his command was the depleted 16th Destroyer Flotilla, which included the leader *Mackay*, under J. P. Wright, with *Worcester*, *Whitshed* and *Walpole*. Combined they were still under normal destroyer flotilla strength. Each ship was well over twenty years old and in most the torpedo tubes had to be hand-worked into position for firing. Normally, both flotillas were used for East coast convoy work, where they were capable of dealing with E-boat skirmishers and U-boats.

Now they were expected under "Fuller" to deal with an enemy battle squadron which might well have defeated any single British fleet then in existence.

Once again, as in the case of Esmonde's Swordfish, the destroyers had been expected to attack only by night, when they could be expected to achieve some tangible success before the enemy properly knew their whereabouts. The plan agreed between Vice-Admiral Ramsay and Captain Pizey involved the crossing of our own mine barrier off the Thames estuary through a specially swept channel. By this route it was hoped that the enemy could be intercepted off the Hinder Banks in the approaches to the Straits. And by good fortune the destroyers were exercising off Harwich when Ramsay's signal was received at 11.45 am.

During the early morning the ships had been at fifteen minutes' notice for steam in accordance with "Fuller" alerts issued before dawn each day. After daylight the notice had been increased to four hours, and on any other day they would have been at their berths and the crews engaged on normal harbour routines. In this event, even the most frantic scramble and the acceptance of sailing with key crew members still ashore could not have put them to sea in under two hours.

On this morning, however, Captain Pizey was able to form up his ships in two divisions — *Campbell*, *Vivacious* and *Worcester* in the First Division; *Mackay*, *Whitshed* and *Walpole* in the Second Division — and set off to intercept at 28 knots.

It was too late to use the planned route. The only possible chance to make contact with the enemy lay in crossing the mine barrier by the shortest possible short cut. With no further hesitation, Captain Pizey led the destroyers into our own minefields.

At 1.18 pm *Walpole* began lagging behind, and eventually signalled that she was unable to maintain speed due to main bearings running hot. She was told to return to harbour. A few minutes later the first air attacks developed when a flight of Ju88 bombers and another of Ju87 dive-bombers on the lookout for British surface forces flew just under the cloud ceiling and dropped a pattern of bombs across *Mackay*.

During this period crews at action stations had been warned of the danger from our mines and those not essential to the actual steaming of the ships lay down at their guns and torpedo tubes, heads facing inboard. It was thought that this would minimise the effect of exploding mines.

It is curious that in these anxious, tense moments, when members of all ships' companies surreptitiously wrote last notes home on grubby bits of paper with stubs of pencils and exchanged them, there was a careless, almost impossibly diffident attitude to the mine danger.

Official records do not, for instance, reveal that one commanding officer thought of a simple method of keeping up morale among men who justifiably considered themselves doomed. He ordered his Yeoman of Signals to pass to the ship ahead a challenge to the captain to play "Battleships" — a popular game in the Navy which can be played by two people only. Receiving an affirmative, the game began with results being passed to the respective crews, who soon either supported their captains or became disgusted at their respective prowess.

With such an example, these crews at least crossed the mine barrier with something to think about other than danger — which achieved the result of high morale.

Yet nothing could be done to minimise the battle ahead. Only luck, skill and constant prayer could be expected to save them from total extinction.

At 2 pm the mine barrier was left behind. At 2.45 the ships were steaming in line ahead at full speed when a flock of aircraft appeared out of the cloud. Behind them a single aircraft turned in the direction of the ships. As it approached guns' crews trained their guns until the order passed down the line:

"Friendly aircraft ahead."

It was a Hampden of Bomber Command coming in low on the starboard bow at *Mackay*. Guns were trained fore and aft again and look-outs switched their attention to more aircraft seen in the distance. Suddenly an officer on *Mackay's* bridge shouted:

"The Hampden has let go bombs."

Even as he said it the bombs fell astern of the destroyer, exploding in her wake and drenching the after-guns' crews with spray. The gunnery officer, fearful that the anti-aircraft crews would open fire, shouted into his telephone control system:

"Check, check, check. Do not open fire. Repeat do not open fire." He paused, then added: "That aircraft is friendly, although it has a funny way of showing it."

The bomber had no intention of leaving them yet. Turning, it came in low again, this time over *Worcester*, and bombs fell on either side, straddling her bridge. Still there was no fire from the destroyers. This attack emptied the bomber, and it headed back into cloud.

Said a *Worcester* sailor sadly: "What's another air force when the lot's against us already."

At 3.17, when visibility was estimated at four miles, *Campbell's* radar picked up the enemy battle fleet at a range of nine and a half miles, and three minutes later Captain Pizey was given the course and speed of the enemy. His signal blinked down the line of ships:

I intend to close the enemy and attack. Once the enemy is engaged ships will attack independently. Good luck.

It was luck that they would need twenty minutes later when gun flashes were seen four miles ahead as the port escort screen came into view with flak guns warding off the first

Beaufort attacks. The destroyers, with a top speed of 28 knots, had reached the enemy at the same time as Coastal Command.

Captain Pizey took *Campbell* in to attack *Gneisenau*. Although ordered to act independently, *Vivacious* and *Worcester* elected to follow him in what was later described as "a model attack". The enemy formation was taken completely by surprise as the little British ships came racing out of the mist, torpedo tubes ready and guns blazing. *Gneisenau*'s captain admitted later that he was so wrapped in concern for the air that his first indication that a surface force was anywhere near came when a shell exploded near his ship's water-line and greeny-yellow smoke-clouds swirled around the bridge.

The three destroyers scattered the E-boats screen and turned about 4000 yards from the enemy battle cruiser to fight a running gun duel — puny pricks against mighty blows. The heavy guns of the enemy formation roared out an angry broadside at this impudent challenge.

Behind the First Division, *Mackay* sighted another huge shadow materialise in the mist — *Prinz Eugen*, then nearly two miles astern of *Gneisenau*. Captain Wright led *Whitshed* into the attack, behind Pizey, as the battle squadron's great guns veered towards them and the broadside cut a swathe through the water fifty feet ahead. The official German report says:[14]

"Both *Prinz Eugen* and *Gneisenau* opened fire with the heavy naval guns. The English destroyers turning on a parallel course engaged the main formation in a running gun battle. They are firing torpedoes, and at the same time the German ships are attacked from the air by torpedo-carriers.

"After the first direct hits on the enemy destroyers — three of the hits as seen from *Gneisenau* cause fires — the *Prinz Eugen* sinks one destroyer and sets a second on fire. The enemy turns

---

[14] A literal translation.

away sharply in order to engage while passing and is almost immediately out of sight in the mist.

"After the enemy has turned away, both ships proceed in order to carry out main task (reach home waters); the German destroyers receive the signal 'Destroyers attack'; and on completion of this task they return to the formation."

Captain Pizey's report reveals a different picture:

"We were engaged by the enemy's main armament as we went in. It seemed incredible that we were not hit. Our aircraft attacked about the same time and a German destroyer came out of the mist to deliver a torpedo attack against *Vivacious* which passed down her side about 15 yards away.

"At 3300 yards the enemy's fire was so heavy that I decided to turn and fire torpedoes. Our luck could not have held out much longer. *Vivacious* turned with me and we fired torpedoes together.

"*Worcester* pressed even closer under a heavy concentration of fire receiving hits and suffering severe damage.

"All ships attacked the leader of the enemy line."

The story of HMS *Worcester* during this classic action is the story of a ship that wouldn't die. As Captain Pizey led the way in to attack, *Worcester* pulled out of line to obtain a clear approach run for her torpedo attack. When *Campbell* and *Vivacious* turned to fire, she went right on in, her captain, Lieutenant-Commander E. C. Coates, oblivious of all else other than the target.

Although only little more than 4000 yards from the enemy his range-finder gave him 5000 so he pressed closer. When the other two destroyers turned, the German gunners switched their attention from the danger past to the danger coming and placed *Worcester* under a concentrated heavy barrage.

Miraculously she reached a range of 3000 yards before turning to fire her torpedo, then, having given prolonged protection to the gallant little ship, luck deserted her. A salvo from the cruiser's heavy guns struck home against *Worcester's* side, shattering her decks and taking away the starboard side of the bridge. Two more salvos hit in rapid succession, exploding inside Nos 1 and 2 Boiler Rooms, bringing the destroyer to a stop.

Screams of wounded, the hiss of steam escaping from the damaged boilers and shouted orders quietened to an agonising silence as slowly the destroyer swung in the tide and presented a broadside-on target to the second enemy ship in line, the menacing *Prinz Eugen*.

The German gunners could take their time about this unexpected opportunity for target practice. Four salvoes of heavy naval gunfire ripped through *Worcester* tearing steel apart, whipping her guns to shreds and tearing great, gaping holes in her side.

Captain Fein of *Gneisenau* said in his report:

"I watched our heavy guns score direct hits on the English destroyer and it seemed to me that she heeled so far over under the impact that she nearly capsized. I ordered our guns to cease fire, as there seemed no point in wasting shells on a ship already sinking. No destroyer, or any ship of that size, could be hit that heavily and survive."

Captain Fein, if he still lives, will probably know better now. Although the punishment inflicted on her should by all accepted standards have been mortal, *Worcester* stayed afloat. She was listing dangerously and on fire fore and aft. Lieutenant-Commander Coates was inclined to share the German captain's view and ordered from the bridge:

"Prepare to abandon ship."

The battle tumult overwhelmed all but the last words of the order and round the ship and down the engine-room, ran the shout "Abandon ship". Those on deck who heard and were under no specific orders gently lifted the wounded into rafts and slid them over the side; those who could still walk or swim were pushed overboard and told to rely on their life-jackets. Rafts and the men in the water drifted slowly away from the staggering ship.

White-hot steam stabbed in huge gushers from the engine-room, mingling with the smoke from the guns and from burning superstructure. Another salvo from the enemy ships wiped out X gun turret, but Y turret kept up firing until the crew fell at their action stations.

Amidships the two pom-poms, the only guns left, continued the action under the control of Sub-Lieutenant J. F. N. Wedge, a young Reserve officer who, suffering from severe shell-shock, still gave his orders. Further aft and before the bridge the Oerlikon guns crews fell dead or wounded across their guns.

The enemy were hitting the ship with every salvo and one explosion blew a group of freshly wounded sailors overboard. The First Lieutenant, Lieutenant J. W. L. Winterbottom, saw their plight and jumped into the sea to save them one by one.

Suddenly the firing ceased and the German battle fleet moved on, content that a sinking ship lay helpless in their wake.

As *Campbell* and *Vivacious* came out from their attack, *Mackay* led in the Second Division through the enemy barrage and fired torpedoes at 3000 yards. Despite *Worcester*'s plight the sea-gods smiled on these destroyers; for again they came out almost unscathed.

It was nearing 4 pm when *Campbell* and *Vivacious* withdrew into the protective mist and sighted a ship in the haze two miles away. On the bridge lookouts and officers trained their glasses and saw what they thought was the last of *Worcester*. The two destroyers raced across to her assistance to find fires raging down her entire length, rafts, floats and men drifting away in the water.

Then the enemy bombers, guided by the Luftwaffe officers aboard the German battle squadron, screamed down to dive-bomb the rescue operations. While their guns blazed at the bomber flights, *Campbell* and *Vivacious* picked up the men in the water and drew alongside the rafts. Captain Pizey's report said:

> When most of the men in the water had been brought aboard *Campbell*, and *Vivacious* was handling the rest, we closed *Worcester* to take her in tow. Picking up the survivors was difficult because of rough weather and the inability of the men to help themselves due to wounds, intense cold and exhaustion.
>
> Somehow *Worcester* was getting her fires under some semblance of control, and we could not help but raise a cheer when she signalled she was able to raise steam to attempt the passage home herself.
>
> The confusion in the air was amazing. During these operations we were beaten up and bombed by both the enemy and our own aircraft.

Understandably in the hazy weather, aircraft which had some difficulty in finding ships, let alone identifying them as hostile or friendly, solved the problem by classing all surface vessels as belonging to the enemy battle fleet. Seeing the three destroyers below, they came down and attacked with bombs, cannon and machine-gun fire.

Captain Wright of *Mackay* said in his report:

> The mixture of aircraft in our vicinity was extraordinary. Low there were large numbers of Me109s and a few Beauforts; a bit higher were Hampdens and Dorniers, Halifaxes and Me110s. In the course of the action we sighted Hampdens, Halifaxes, Beauforts, Wellingtons, Manchesters, Whirlwinds, Spitfires, Dorniers, Me110s, Me109s, FW190s, Ju88s, Ju87s and He111s.
>
> Some enemy aircraft thought we were friendly; some of our own thought we were hostile. We, on our part, opened fire on aircraft later recognised as friendly. The aircraft on both sides must have found the situation rather confusing.

During the rescue operations, three Beauforts came in low through the mist and fired torpedoes at *Campbell* and *Vivacious*. These were the three from Leuchars which had lost their squadron during the flight across the North Sea.

There was no reluctance on the part of the destroyer's gunners to fire now. They put up an extremely accurate barrage at first, then recognised the aircraft as friendly, and ceased firing. The torpedo bombers were allowed to approach and drop their loads unchallenged.

Captain Pizey's report said:

> While standing by *Worcester Campbell* and *Vivacious* drove off several air attacks. At 16.15 three Beauforts came in low, the second being seen to fire a torpedo. The other two probably did, but were not seen. One torpedo was heard approaching on the Asdic, and although there were rafts of wounded alongside, I reluctantly had to go full speed astern and the torpedo passed ahead of me.
>
> We fortunately were able to come up to the rafts again and pick up the occupants.

Mackay and *Whitshed* re-joined *Campbell* and *Vivacious* after delivering their attack and the four ships grouped round *Worcester* to shepherd her home. It seemed astonishing that she had not yet sunk and there were few among the flotilla who thought she was likely to reach harbour. But the plucky little ship refused to die; she staggered along in company at eight knots while *Campbell* led the way back home, choosing to cross the mine-barrier off Harwich, as they had done on the way out.

The wounded needed urgent attention, and the Commander-in-Chief, Nore, sent out four Hunt Class destroyers to escort *Worcester* and enable the tired and damaged flotilla to return at full speed. These destroyers failed to contact *Worcester* in the twilight and she was left to make the last stages of the trip alone. The next morning she limped into Harwich, desperately hurt but still alive. The crews of every ship in harbour lined their decks to send out cheer after cheer as the gallant destroyer, turning back the tugs dispatched to help her, steamed slowly and unaided into her berth. The greatest battle fleet the enemy had been able to muster for the entire war had failed to sink her. She earned for herself that day a soubriquet that stayed with her for the remainder of the war — *Worcester*, the ship that wouldn't die.

Esmonde's Swordfish were expected to be destroyed. Pizey's destroyers were the "last-chance" gamble which it was also thought might end in total destruction. Instead, by good fortune the destroyers came through without loss, and with only *Worcester* seriously damaged. Although luck had played the greater share, Captain Pizey and the officers and men under him blessed the weather that day. For in the protective mist they were able to make their attack runs unseen until the last minute.

There is no evidence, however, to show that the weather played any part in the Admiralty's decision to order the destroyers into the attack. They did so in the full expectation of severe casualties.

It is nothing if not astonishing that in the ten months which had passed the operation was never considered of sufficient importance to ensure that the destroyer force was adequate rather than impossibly inadequate.

> *Their Lordships concur with Captain Pizey's bold decision to cross the mine barrier in order to intercept and contact with the enemy was rendered possible as a result of his sound appreciation of the situation.*

This verdict by Their Lordships, which also referred to *Campbell's* action as a model attack, continued:

> It was pressed home very well in the face of enemy gunfire. *Campbell* and *Vivacious* escaped damage due to Captain Pizey's faultless judgment and handling of the ships plus a modicum of luck.

From the Board of Admiralty this was almost hysterical praise. Their Lordships expect warships to do their duty, and if that duty leads to success they are never surprised, nor inspired to praise it unduly. Reports of the action are normally analysed, and more than one commander who thinks he has done rather well finds that under expert analysis he might have done better.

In this instance, Captain Pizey could be well pleased that he had not incurred Their Lordships' displeasure in any part of his action; in fact he could assume that they were both relieved and delighted that he returned at all.

The destroyer attack had two unexpected consequences. The first was an inter-Service exchange which merely reflected the bitterness which the Channel dash let loose in Whitehall.

Referring to the attack on *Campbell* and *Vivacious* by Beauforts while they were picking up *Worcester*'s wounded, a letter from the Admiralty to the Air Ministry said:

> We think that the unwarranted attack on HM Destroyers by three Beaufort torpedo bombers on February 12th demands explanation. The Senior Officer's report is herewith attached.

The Air Ministry, probably with a more realistic approach but with an utter lack of tact, replied:

> Low clouds, poor visibility and generally bad weather conditions prevailed and a certain amount of confusion was inevitable. The three aircraft concerned believed their target to be enemy warships.

If the Air Ministry thought the Admiralty were being a little unreasonable, they had ample justification. While the weather could be blamed for most things there were contributing reasons for the mistake. Of these the most important was that the Admiralty had not warned any of the Commands concerned that our destroyers were in the target area, although they would have known from the original plan that surface attacks would be made.

The second feature of this attack concerned Captain Pizey's decision to risk crossing the East Coast mine barrier when steaming to intercept and on return when he was anxious to have the wounded treated in hospital as quickly as possible.

In fact no mines existed in the area. For an Admiralty investigation showed: "these mines were non-existent because they had been cleared several days previously. The relevant signal to this effect had not yet been sent and was not in fact sent until later that same night."

The fact that Captain Pizey did decide to cross the minefield was indeed a "bold decision", as he was not aware that it had been cleared. Apart from a departmental report to this effect there is no mention of this in any overall document of the destroyer action.

Worcester absorbed tremendous punishment. Her bows were burnt out, mast and funnels shot away, ammunition lockers blown up, boiler-rooms holed; her bridge was riddled, wireless room wrecked, hull holed above the water-line and extensive damage was done generally by explosives, splinter holes and flooding.

Four men were killed and nineteen wounded.

Meanwhile, the massed air assaults of Bomber and Fighter Commands were gathering momentum.

CHAPTER 12: A QUIET DAY OF THE WAR

Bomber Command's operational order of May 1st, 1941, laid down the conditions under which the Command could launch an effective offensive against the enemy ships passing up Channel, or even through the Dover Straits. This order demanded suitable cloud-cover in areas where Fighter Command could not be expected to operate and, as a result of the original Air Ministry letter warning of a possible Brest breakout, took into account the possibility of a daylight passage through the Straits. It is said:

> If the Channel dash is attempted it may take place at any time without prior warning being possible. The ships will be attacked by surface craft and aircraft by day. It is not intended that aircraft (bombers) should attack by night. Unless suitable cloud cover is available, attacks will not be ordered except in areas where Fighter Command can give protection.
>
> It is unlikely that the enemy will pass the Straits of Dover in daylight. If he does it will be necessary to take advantage of the opportunity afforded by the fighter screen in the area to attack with the largest possible striking force.

In general terms there was no ambiguity in this plan until the part which dealt with the bomb-loads.

> Stirlings to carry maximum loads of 2000-lb. of armour-piercing made up of 500-lb. semi-armour-piercing bombs. All other aircraft to carry maximum loads of 500-lb. semi-armour-piercing bombs.

This type of bomb needed a minimum of 7000 feet from which to be dropped with any hope of real effect. It would seem to the uninitiated that such a height might well be a vain hope over the Channel in winter time.

When "Operation Fuller" was put into effect, Bomber Command placed nearly 300 bombers of all types throughout the country at a state of two hours' readiness. This meant that the aircraft were bombed up and lay at their dispersal points; the crews were fully briefed and waiting together as crews on the airfields. Such a plan deprived the Command of a large force which would normally be used in nightly raids over enemy territory; as far as these aircraft were concerned all training and operational work came to a standstill.

It was a situation which could not be allowed to remain in force for long, and, when consequent paralysis began seeping through the Command, Sir Richard Peirse asked the Air Ministry on February 6th to be released from all obligations under "Fuller". The Ministry naturally replied that before such a grave depletion of the plan's forces could be permitted, Sir Richard would have to consult the Admiralty.

The following day Bomber Command placed the request before the Admiralty for approval, a move which caused utter consternation among the naval planners. The degree of danger of the ships breaking out of Brest had not become less, said the Admiralty, but, in fact, had increased and would continue to increase as the tides became more favourable.

The Command weighed this against the principal task of maintaining the bomber offensive against Germany and promptly made up its own mind concerning "Fuller". Two-thirds of the force were released and made available to operational units or to training squadrons, while 100 bombers were held inside the "Fuller" organisation, but their state of readiness was reduced to four hours' notice. On this call only fifty per cent of the force were bombed up, the rest could be used for tests and training and the crews were supposed to remain on duty — a term which was interpreted differently by each squadron leader or station commander.

After the circulation of Sir Philip Joubert's appreciation of the 8th, however, Sir Richard had second thoughts and modified the order to the extent of keeping the 100 bombers "bombed up".

At no time was the Admiralty, predominant partner in the bi-Service "Fuller", informed of Bomber Command's decisions in this respect.

Between February 2nd and 9th the Command laid ninety-eight mines on a specified area off the Friesian Islands. The Brest ships had been a headache to the Command for so long it would seem natural for the HQ Staff to be interested after one reconnaissance on the 11th showed *Scharnhorst*, *Gneisenau* and *Prinz Eugen* all out of drydock and repair yards and lying in fuelling wharves. Six destroyers were also in harbour. It appeared that the boom defences were still in place.

At 9 am on February 12th Sir Richard reviewed the Command's activities for the next twenty-four hours. The weather was not encouraging, so he ruled out the possibility of being called upon under "Fuller". It was to him "one of the quiet days of the war".

The peace then at Bomber Command's headquarters was disturbed but not destroyed at 11.27 am, when reports drifted in from other Commands that something big was coming up the Channel. The final destruction of the headquarters calm came at 11.40, when Sir Richard Peirse was formally warned that *Scharnhorst*, *Gneisenau* and *Prinz Eugen* were approaching the

Straits of Dover. It was further aggravated by an Air Ministry signal to all three Air Commands at 12.32 pm which said:

> *Scharnhorst* and *Gneisenau* reported in Channel about 16 miles west cf Le Touquet at 1105/12. Abnormal enemy air activity reported. Maximum forces to be employed as early as possible to destroy enemy ships and aircraft. This unique opportunity to be exploited to utmost.

Operationally fit aircraft and crews available throughout the country at that moment numbered 310. Of these, fifty were Whitleys considered unsuitable for daylight bombing operations and a number of Wellingtons were snow-bound and unable to take off. The final available figure for possible takeoff was reduced to 240, which included the hundred kept at four hours' notice under the Command's private and confidential "Fuller". This was the "utmost" called for by the Air Ministry to take advantage of a "unique opportunity"!

Despite the state of the weather, the Command was now faced with compulsory operations at sea, and accordingly telephone contact was opened with Coastal Command to coordinate bomber and torpedo attacks, and with Fighter Command to arrange suitable escorts.

The state of the weather was 7-10ths to 10-10ths cloud, with base at 2000 feet and sometimes as little as 700 feet — most unsuitable for bombing. Moreover the visibility was estimated at not more than a mile, and this was expected to become worse as the day wore on.

In these circumstances, Sir Richard Peirse decided there was little chance of his Command being able to cripple the heavy ships. His only hope of doing this lay in high-altitude bombing with armour-piercing bombs. That course was more or less impossible because with low cloud-base these bombs could not be dropped from sufficient height to pierce armour. The only alternative was to arm the bombers with general-purpose bombs which would explode on impact and create death and destruction over a wide area of deck-space without penetrating the steel plate.

Under these conditions it soon became evident to the Command that the bombloads of the 100 aircraft standing by at four hours' notice had to be switched while the remaining 140 available aircraft were alerted and bombed up.

Accordingly orders were issued that general-purpose bombs were to be exchanged for armour-piercing to the greatest extent possible, but that the departure of the first wave of bombers was not to be held up because of the change-over. It was to some extent hoped that the few bombers carrying armour-piercing might find cloud-breaks at 7000 feet from which they could attack effectively.

In principle, however, Sir Richard considered that his Command's role that afternoon would be possibly to damage the enemy with the blast of general-purpose bombs and time these attacks so as to cause the maximum distraction to German crews while the torpedo bombers approached.

Telephone consultations were held with Coastal Command, from whom it was learned that the Thorney Island torpedo bombers were leaving Manston at 1.30 pm, and his naval liaison officer was told by the Admiralty that the Swordfish would attack as quickly as possible — about 1 pm.

With the most alerted bombers at four hours' notice, armed with the wrong type of bombs and the crews dispersed about a variety of duties unconnected with "Fuller", it was immediately clear that there would be little hope of co-ordinating attacks to provide the necessary assistance to the Royal Navy. It was equally apparent that only the later attacks by the torpedo bombers would benefit by the presence of a bomber force.

Therefore it was decided to send into the air the greatest number of aircraft ready at 2.30 pm, regardless of the type of bombs they carried. Nearly four hours, then, were to elapse between the sighting of the enemy and the first Bomber Command attack. It was accepted that the second attack could not develop over the target until 4 pm, by which time the enemy battle fleet would have drawn out of range of fighters.

At 2.20 pm the first wave of bombers took off for the target area — seventy-three aircraft drawn from all over the country, some of which were among the hundred standing by for "Fuller". No attempt was made to combine this force into a formation, instead the pilots headed out to sea towards the enemy either singly or in pairs.

The Coastal Command Beauforts with which the attack was supposed to have been co-ordinated were at that time bothered and bewildered at Manston.

General fighter cover in the area had been established and the first bombers arrived on the target area at nearly 3 p.m. It seems that from then onwards each pilot was forced to find either *Scharnhorst* or *Gneisenau* in the low prevailing visibility and make an individual attack. As *Scharnhorst* was thirty miles astern of the main formation, *Prinz Eugen* was thought to be the battle cruiser, and many of the pilots pressed home courageous attacks on her despite the intensity of the flak.

It was not until the main force of Bomber Command reported ready, still with an even distribution of armour-piercing and general-purpose bombs, that there was any hope of a concerted attack. In this wave 134 assorted bombers crossed the North Sea to the target area as the last of the first wave were returning home, most of them not having sighted the heavy units at all.

Once again the weather intervened, and the second force arrived in dribbles over the target area at 4 pm. Of these only a few found the enemy battle fleet, and unfortunately the majority were armed with armour-piercing bombs. One pilot sighted *Gneisenau* and flew low over her to ensure correct identification. Then he made repeated attempts to climb high enough to release his bombs, but each time entered cloud and lost sight of his target.

He was joined by two more bombers, and the three decided to attack from below the cloud-base. The bombs of the first aircraft could not be released, the second missed from 1500 feet and the third from 200 feet.

At 4.15 pm Bomber Command's third wave of thirty-five bombers took off, and reached the enemy ships, then well out of range of short-range fighters, at 5.50 pm. Most of them lost their way and returned to base. The last of these bomber attempts was made at 6.15, in darkness, rain and mist.

During this phase of the battle *Scharnhorst* had repaired her mine damage sufficiently to set off after the main battle fleet at full speed. She was attacked repeatedly by bombers which were operating too far to the south. In the absence of any coherent story of the aircraft attacks, the official report of her commander, Captain Hoffman, shows how powerful the offensive seemed in German eyes.

From 1500 to 1815 bomber and torpedo-carrying planes attacked the ships almost incessantly. The machines came singly, partly in groups of two or three and these mostly in open formation. Owing to visibility closing in they could be bombarded for only a short space of time. Yet they were all bombarded with varying degrees of success.

Owing to the occasional mists and low clouds it was not always possible to tell if new bomber waves came with every approach or if it was the same aircraft repeatedly trying again. All the planes which attacked the ship were forced to turn away before dropping their bombs due to heavy and accurate flak.

The enemy had the advantage as poor weather made accurate AA fire not always possible. On occasions bombers were permitted to approach almost to dropping point before being engaged. But at the first flak they usually broke off the action.

Although we were for most of this time without escort, having lost our stand-by E-boats, we were not at any time seriously engaged by enemy air or surface forces. Only a few men on the upper deck were wounded by splinters. Three men, however, suffered slight injuries from a torpedo-carrying aircraft of the Beaufort type which came low across us spraying the upper deck with machine-gun fire. The pilot and crew of this machine must have been brave men to face our flak for so long. They were not seen to drop their torpedo.

The fighter cover kept most of the aircraft from the target area and only a few of the number which must have taken off ever reached us.

Few indeed of the first two waves found the enemy battle fleet. There was even less hope of the third force making contact. By 5 pm the enemy had been split up. *Prinz Eugen* took evasive action to dodge the Beaufort attack and lost contact with *Gneisenau*. A few E-boats and torpedo boats maintaining station on her were also lost. *Gneisenau* continued on course with the destroyer screen only in sight.

In three hours and fifteen minutes 242 bombers took off to attack the enemy, of which thirty-nine sighted the heavy ships and 188 returned without making contact. Fifteen bombers were lost and another crashed while landing at base.

The "unique opportunity" had in some way eluded them — but for the Commandant as a whole there was no one who could agree that February 12th was one of the "quiet days of the war".

Fighter Command aircraft were the last British forces to break contact with the enemy. From 12.20 pm, when the first squadrons took off to rendezvous with Esmonde's Swordfish, the Command maintained constant sorties, for which both sides paid heavily.

The Command's role in "Fuller" had been vested in No11 Group under the Air Officer Commanding, Air Vice-Marshal Leigh-Mallory. He was authorised to draw on No 10 Group for reinforcements. His area of operations extended from Lowestoft in the north to the Isle of Wight in the south, and to the planners it seemed that his forces would be mostly affected should the dash be attempted.

At dawn on the 12th the strength of the Group was twenty-one Spitfire squadrons and four Hurricane squadrons. At intervals as the day wore on these were reinforced by three Spitfire squadrons from No10 Group and two from No12 Group. In addition, four squadrons from No12 Group became accidentally involved in the battle.

The total number of squadrons upon which Leigh-Mallory could call for his offensive was thirty-four, numbering in all between 550 and 600 fighters.

After the alarm and swift departure of the Biggin Hill and Hornchurch wings to meet Esmonde, Leigh-Mallory telephoned Coastal and Bomber Commands to find out what their plans entailed and at what times they would require fighter protection.

It was agreed that he should arrange for fighter cover extending from Dover to the constantly moving battlefield.

The exception to this rule was the Swordfish operation, which was settled between Dover and the Group headquarters.

After his telephone discussions with Sir Philip Joubert and Sir Richard Peirse, Leigh-Mallory considered it unlikely that his fighters would be required by either command until 2 pm at the earliest. He decided to conserve his aircraft for these operations while at the same time mounting attacks against the battle fleet's escorts in the intervening period.

On his orders ten Hurricane fighter bombers of 607 Squadron left Manston at 12.40 pm on their first sortie. They failed to locate the enemy and swept down through the Straits to Boulogne, where they attacked and damaged four small ships, probably marker boats returning to harbour after the passing of the battle squadron. Shore batteries opened up and one Hurricane was shot down.

At 1.18 pm eight cannon-firing Hurricanes escorted by a squadron of fighters took off from Manston to attack the E-boat screens. Again they failed to find the enemy and encountered light forces between Gravelines and Dunkirk. Heavy fire was exchanged, with damage to both sides. No aircraft were lost.

At 1.40 pm another squadron of cannon-firing Hurricanes, escorted by a squadron of fighters, left Tangmere to find the elusive E-boats. This third attempt succeeded and the outer screen of the battle fleet was engaged. Four aircraft and three pilots were lost in this operation.

Two o'clock came and went without sign of the Bomber or Coastal forces, so another offensive was launched by the Hurricanes of 607 Squadron. They were escorted by two squadrons of fighters. On their way to the German forces they were set upon by two large formations of enemy fighters. The fighter bombers were separated from their escorts in the general dogfight and went on to lose their way over the North Sea. While searching for signs of the enemy's passage they sighted two large enemy merchant ships, which they attacked. Three of these fighter-bombers failed to return.

While these operations were being carried out, Leigh-Mallory dispatched a fighter force to cover the Coastal Command Beaufort detachment from Thorney Island, due to leave Manston at 1.30. The Kenley Wing of three squadrons failed to find the Beauforts and proceeded to the last known position of the enemy. Sweeping northwards, they encountered the enemy "umbrella", but one squadron managed to get below it and attack the E-boats with cannon. This time four enemy aircraft were destroyed.

No11 Group's next task was to provide suitable escort for Pizey's destroyers. This operation was entrusted to a Whirlwind squadron from No12 Group, which took off in three flights during the period 1.10 to 2.29 pm. None of these flights contacted the destroyers, probably because of Captain Pizey's decision to divert from the planned interception route. The Whirlwinds' search led close to the enemy and they were heavily engaged by the Luftwaffe. Four Whirlwinds were shot down and their pilots lost.

The Command's most concentrated effort was mounted between 2.05 and 3.05 pm to cover the first of the Beaufort torpedo-bomber attacks and the first wave of bombers, both expected to take place during those periods. During this hour fifteen squadrons of fighters were sent to the target area as follows:

The North Weald Wing left at 2.05 pm and encountered fifty enemy aircraft over the target area. In the ensuing battle one enemy aircraft was destroyed for no loss. Next, the Debden Wing of two squadrons left at 2.09 pm. and ran into more than

100 enemy fighters off Dunkirk. The uneven battle raged for twenty minutes, and ended with two enemy aircraft being shot down without loss to the Wing.

The three fighter squadrons of the Biggin Hill Wing took off on their second sortie at 2.45, but passage across the sea was a continuous battle which was broken off without casualties on either side. Also taking off at this time on their second trip of the day were the Hornchurch squadrons, reinforced by two more squadrons from No12 Group. The enemy was not sighted during this sortie, and, astonishingly, the four squadrons returned having fired not one shot in anger.

Three squadrons of No10 Group left at 2.40 pm and flew right over the enemy formation, before being heavily engaged by the Luftwaffe. Two Me109s were shot down for the loss of three of our aircraft and their pilots.

No12 Group also supplied three squadrons to cover the withdrawal of the first bomber wave. These fighters patrolled 60 miles to the east of the Norfolk coast and saw a large number of bombers returning, but no enemy fighters.

Overall, the Fighter picture shows that with nearly 600 fighters available on paper, 398 were actually dispatched to attack the enemy. Of these seventeen were shot down. One 600-ton vessel and an E-boat were claimed as sunk and eight assorted escort craft damaged. Sixteen enemy fighters were shot down, three more probably destroyed and seventeen damaged.

The last aircraft of Fighter Command assigned to shadowing duties was recalled when darkness and the weather ruled out further attacks by either surface or air forces.

The men who flew the planes and manned the little ships had fought magnificently: faced the odds indomitably and suffered death equally. Yet the casualty toll for the known results at that time struck a sombre chord.

The Royal Navy had lost a squadron of six Swordfish, a destroyer had been so severely punished she would be out of action for several months and the MTBs had been cut to shreds. Thirteen Fleet Air arm officers and men had been killed and four of *Worcester*'s crew had died. Forty more officers and men suffered injuries ranging from grave to light.

Seventeen fighters had been shot down with one pilot saved; Coastal Command lost three Beauforts and two Hudsons with their crews; of the Bomber forces, nine Hampdens, four Wellingtons and two Blenheims failed to return.

Apart from the Luftwaffe losses, two torpedo boats — *Jaguar* and *T-13* — were damaged by bombs, and several German sailors were seriously wounded by bomb splinters and machine-gun fire.

What had the slender forces of "Fuller" achieved for their appalling losses? Had the enemy escaped without a scratch?

The battle fleet was nearing home. There was one more move to make.

At 11 pm that night twenty bombers took off, at the Admiralty's request, to lay mines in the mouth of the Elbe. Twelve of these aircraft succeeded in laying their mines and returned safely. At Whitehall the hopes of a frustrated, angry, resentful staff waited impatiently for the final chapter.[15]

When Vice-Admiral Ciliax leapt aboard the destroyer Z-29 he felt that the fleet's chances of continuing the dash unscathed were remote. Misfortune had struck for the first

---

[15] That evening Group Captain Gleave took off from Manston feeling "very bloody-minded". Filled with anger and grief he nearly flew into the sea himself. It was, he told me, "the most depressing flight I had ever made".

time, and might well strike again. A few miles ahead, altering course to avoid torpedoes and manoeuvring from the dangerous approach of bombers, his squadron was holding its high speed but reducing progress over the ground.

In shallow waters, the powerful thrusts of propellers produced only 29 knots where in deeper water the average speed had been 31. On *Prinz Eugen*'s quarterdeck the crews of light antiaircraft guns had to abandon action stations and scamper for safety, as her stern was sucked so deep that the water boiled in foaming waves across the deck.

Z-29 caught up with the main formation at 4.20 pm and Ciliax ordered her captain to take station at the head of the column. A small anti-aircraft shell exploded amidships through over-heating and a piece of shrapnel cut through an oil feedpipe, reducing the destroyer's speed to 25 knots. Once again the German commander was forced to change ships in mid-battle.

Another destroyer, *Hermann Schoemann*, was ordered alongside, but the rough seas made it impossible for the two ships to lay alongside each other long enough for the transfer without risk of serious damage. A remarkable sailor, Ciliax had *Z-29*'s cutter lowered, and with both ships stopped, fighters, bombers and torpedo bombers overhead, he was ceremoniously piped down the rope ladder into the waiting boat, his staff following with some trepidation. He huddled in the stern while the little boat rocked its way across the gap to *Hermann Schoemann*. He climbed the rope ladder up her side with remarkable agility and was piped aboard. On his curt order, the destroyer picked up full speed and headed for the fleet, leaving *Z-29* to make her own way to harbour.

His fears concerning *Scharnhorst* were quickly dispelled when her great dark shape loomed from the haze, shrouded in gunsmoke, with aircraft attacking at her stern. She beat off the attackers as she came abreast of the destroyers and exchanged signals. *Hermann Schoemann* formed up ahead of her and led the way back to the advancing battle fleet.

The Channel dash was taking a favourable shape for the Germans. Now running up the Dutch coast, they had been steaming at maximum speed for eighteen hours, passed through the Straits without damage, warded off the MTB attack, destroyed the Swordfish squadron, broken up Pizey's destroyer attacks and beaten off intermittent bomber and torpedo attacks for several hours.

The mine danger had always been of primary concern and the damage to *Scharnhorst* not unexpected. Fortunately it had been possible to repair her temporarily, so that after thirty minutes she had been able to resume full speed.

Then two events happened which made everything doubtful again.

CHAPTER 13: MIDNIGHT — END OF A DAY

The last British aircraft had vanished into the darkness at 6.15. Ten minutes later the scattered remnants of the Luftwaffe "umbrella" returned to Belgian and French airfields. "The Beginning of Spring" had become the dawn of a German naval summer; not for 300 years had such an operation been tried; history recorded no success. At Le Touquet, Fighter General Adolf Galland signalled his congratulations to the Luftwaffe fighters and bombers. Their role had ended, the ships were protected now by weather and by nightfall. The champagne could run; the Führer's blessings and medals would come later. Only Vice-Admiral Ciliax in the destroyer *Hermann Schoemann*, of all the commanders, fought back the temptation to rejoice openly. Wily, skilful sailor that he was, he could not make up his accounts until the last bill had been paid.

Ahead lay the Friesian Islands, marking the approach to German home waters. To one side were the German minefield defences against the British submarines; between lay a long, narrow bottleneck long believed by the British to be a vital target for aircraft minelayers. He would like to pass through this narrow sea corridor safely before permitting the great battle fleet to cheer its own achievement.

Ciliax's orders forbade the use of R/T or wireless until all ships reached the mouth of the Elbe. For more than two hours the vast armada had been scattered, the three heavy ships spread down the route each about ten miles apart and escorts groping their way through the thick drizzle of the night in small groups, unsure of their positions and fearful of running into their own and British minefields.

Over each ship lay a lethargic pall: the strain of the past twenty-one hours weighing heavily on officers and men. Now came the additional burden of sailing in confined waters without lights and knowing that on every side other darkened shapes were feeling their way homeward on the final sprint.

Gneisenau, making a good 27 knots in waters where she should normally have sailed at ten, stumbled across the marker boats lying off the Friesian Islands, where the route turned sharply eastwards for the run up to Terschelling and the Elbe. Thankfully Captain Fein gave the order to alter course and the great ship heeled over between the markers and headed down the last lap.

Eleven minutes later — at 7.55 pm — a brilliant flash bathed the ship in a pale glow for a fraction of a second, then a tremendous explosion rent the silence. The battle cruiser shuddered under the impact and limped slowly to a stop. Another mine had been struck.

Damage-repair parties swarmed below to investigate the extent of the wound. She lay drifting in the tides only six miles from Terschelling. Half an hour later the gaping rent in her bottom near the stern was blocked by a steel collision mat, and with water-pumps operating, *Gneisenau* picked up speed to resume her passage.

Well after midnight she steamed into the Heligoland Bight — the first of the battle fleet to reach sanctuary. At 7 am the great ship anchored off the Elbe and, as the noise of the anchor chain running out ceased and the captain rang "Finished with engines" on the bridge telegraph, a great cheer welled up from her ship's company. She was damaged, but she was home.

Prinz Eugen was the next. Since 7.30 pm she had groped blindly along the Terschelling banks at eight knots, lying well inside the established route.

At Terschelling the cruiser fixed her position accurately and increased once again to full speed. Shortly before dawn she pulled up alongside *Gneisenau*, more cheers ringing out from tired crews as the second anchor dropped on the Channel Dash.

The last of the three, the flagship *Scharnhorst*, lay well back, turning past the marker boats at the Friesians at 9.14 pm. In *Hermann Schoemann*, then leading, Vice-Admiral Ciliax stayed on the bridge, intermittently casting anxious eyes astern. A quarter of an hour later his nagging fears were justified. A huge explosion rocked the battle cruiser and for the second time during the dash she came to a stop, hit by mines.

Ciliax decided he could not leave her. While the repair parties worked under arc lamps, the destroyer circled protectively around the battle cruiser, ready to engage shadowing surface units.

Scharnhorst had suffered greater damage this time and it was not until midnight that she could signal:

> *Am capable of proceeding at maximum speed of 12 knots. Consider tugs will be necessary to assist entry into harbour.*

Thankfully, Ciliax ordered his flagship to proceed independently to Wilhelmshaven, then 60 miles to the west, and took *Hermann Schoemann* into the Bight.

Aboard *Gneisenau* and *Prinz Eugen*, jubilation was tempered by the lack of any knowledge concerning *Scharnhorst* or Vice-Admiral Ciliax. Throughout the long night most of the crews slept for the first time in more than twenty-four hours. But aboard both ships were those officers who paced the quarterdecks, peering thoughtfully into the night. There could be no victory without *Scharnhorst*, no hero without Ciliax. Hooters and fog-bells were rung at two-minute intervals to tell any ship approaching of the anchorage.

At dawn a small shape came bustling through the swirling mists, hooter blowing plaintively. Men tumbled from their bunks aboard the anchored ships. They lined the guard-rails, filled with rising hopes and gazed at the approaching shape expectantly. A signal lamp flashed the news that *Scharnhorst* had survived and was already approaching port. Suddenly there was a shout, followed by a spontaneous chorus of cheers which rose in crescendo as the shadow of the *Hermann Schoemann* materialised and the rattle of anchor chains broke through the early morning air. The "Ugly Sisters" fleet had arrived. The German admiral received his captains for a victory celebration as he sent a signal to Berlin saying:

> *It is my duty to inform you that Operation Cerberus has been successfully completed. Lists of damage and casualties follow.*

The Channel Dash had ended — the casualties suffered were negligible, but what of the damage sustained by the battle cruisers? *Scharnhorst* had shipped more than 1000 tons of water and her port engine had broken down completely. *Gneisenau* had ripped her bottom and a propeller shaft had been thrown out of line. These were apparent wounds. Only drydock inspections would reveal the full extent of the injuries.

In Ciliax's cabin each captain handed him a copy of their official reports for the past twenty-four hours and, while the events of the day were still vividly implanted on his mind, Ciliax wrote his own report to Admiral Raeder and Hitler.

Now that the three ships have put into German estuaries [he wrote] the Operation Cerberus is ended. With it closes one day of the war at sea, a day which will probably go down as one of the most daring in the naval history of this war. In spite of the damage sustained by *Scharnhorst* and *Gneisenau*, it can be said that the success achieved was above all expectations.

All three ships reached their goal and the enemy, when they attacked, sustained considerable damage both in the air and at sea. The damage to the battle cruisers was not the result of spontaneous counter-measures especially introduced for this particular operation, but much more attributable to the general dangers connected with the navigation of mine infested waters.

The weather, which I have never considered decisive for the carrying out of the operation, developed unfavourably for us, and yet was advantageous to the enemy.

West of the Straits of Dover was calm, with good visibility, and only overcast in part which favoured enemy reconnaissance as well as attacks by dive-bombers or such like if the occasion arose. East of the Straits, when the formation had been located by the enemy as expected, and had concentrated his air attacks and other attacks, the wind and sea decreased the efficiency of the escort vessels, increased the chances of success by enemy torpedo-carrying aircraft and light forces; the decreasing cloud and visibility favoured enemy bombing attacks while at the same time increasingly prejudicing our own fighter activity.

The very detailed briefing before leaving Brest was fully justified; it was made desirable because the needs of security made open discussion impossible. Therefore commanders had to be ordered not to open their secret envelopes until at sea and had to be briefed on what to expect without actually being told what the operation was about.

In spite of this, hardly any further orders were required en route and instead I was able to concentrate entirely on the navigational and tactical leadership of the formation. In that respect, the operation is, in my opinion, a perfect textbook example of what can be achieved by the strict maintenance of security.

The enemy betrayed his surprise to the advantage of our formation by throwing in his air forces precipitously and without plan. For the failure of the enemy Air Force to reach the target during the afternoon and evening in spite of the *extreme determination shown in their first torpedo attack*, we have to thank the ship-borne flak and the fine services of our fighter cover.

After this there was a gap of some two hours or more without any attacks from the enemy and which gave us a decisive breather during which we increased our distance from the enemy and the weather deteriorated. There is no explanation from our side for this delay in the enemy's actions.

Three significant points emerged from this report — the deep impression made on the Admiral Commanding Battleships by the attack of Esmonde's Swordfish, later described in the German War Diary as "the mothball attack of a handful of ancient planes piloted by men whose bravery surpasses any other action by either side that day"; the fact that the weather was never considered decisive for success or failure, and that a vital two-hour gap in the attacks existed which might well have decided the outcome.

These facts were not lost in London, where in Service circles that night a peculiar reluctance to face the next day was not only apparent but in the Admiralty War Room was quietly referred to by a staff officer as "the day of reckoning".

At 1 am on the 13th, as the enemy ships were making their way independently towards the Elbe, Admiral Sir Dudley Pound,

First Sea Lord, lifted the private telephone which connected him with 10 Downing Street. Around him, several senior staff officers gazed intently at maps on the War Room walls, not caring to watch his face.

"I'm afraid, sir," the Admiral said, "I must report that the enemy battle cruisers should by now have reached the safety of their home waters."

He was silent while the waiting officers tried to imagine what the Prime Minister was saying. It must have been brief, for quickly the receiver was replaced and at an inquiring look from another Admiral present, Sir Dudley said:

"I think there's going to be some trouble about this. The Prime Minister was quiet for a bit. He said quite simply: 'Why?' Then he put the phone down."

That question by Winston Churchill to his First Sea Lord was to resound through the country the next morning when all sections of public opinion, regardless of politics, combined to give vent to the shock and sense of disaster which fell across the nation in the wake of the Channel Dash. It rebounded from America and from the Dominions and even from the neutral nations where British power at sea was traditionally regarded as supreme. Without exception, great national and provincial newspapers joined with *The Times* in voicing indignant protests that this "mortifying blow to our pride in seapower" had been permitted to happen.

Simmering resentment spread through the factories and war industries, where workers' meetings passed resolutions condemning the Government's handling of the war. Valuable man-hours were lost and the Minister of Labour, Ernest Bevin, reported that war production had been interrupted in the days immediately following the dash.

Aggravating the position and delivering a further blow to a nation already suffering a severe blow to its prestige, was the German propaganda machine, which chortled happily: "The dying British nation no longer possesses the power or authority to prevent strangers removing flowers from her front garden."

Throughout the 13th the Government, and particularly the Prime Minister, came under blistering attacks from Tories, Socialists and Liberals alike.

Two days later Singapore fell. To Churchill, his mind embracing the grand strategy of war now encircling the globe, the fall of this great British eastern bastion, with the tremendous losses in equipment and men, was of far greater import, making a deeper incision on the slender skin of Allied defences. But to the British public, Singapore was mostly legend separated from reality by thousands of miles and several continents.

The sailing of an enemy battle fleet within sight of the English coast and through the Straits of Dover had infinitely more meaning; how such a flagrantly impudent gesture by the enemy had been allowed to succeed preoccupied the entire nation.

Leader-writers called for explanations and demanded the appointment of a Royal Commission of Inquiry.

Behind all this resentment grew an alarming suspicion which was too invidious to be ignored. The U-boat war was raging in the Atlantic, with honours passing time after time to the enemy. If his surface units could challenge our battle fleets with impunity, was the Navy, like the Army, going to prove inadequate to defend England against the still possible invasion?

In the Commons, where the Channel dash had already been described as a "major blunder", criticisms of the Board of

Admiralty and the Air Staff came out into the open. Under such pressure, the Prime Minister could hold out no longer. Referring to these days in his memoirs, Winston Churchill drew attention to the surrender of Singapore and said:

> But even before this, on February 12th an episode of minor importance as I judged it, but arousing even greater wrath and distress among the public, had occurred. The battle cruisers, *Scharnhorst* and *Gneisenau*, with the cruiser *Prinz Eugen*, had escaped from Brest and made their way up Channel running the gauntlet of the batteries of Dover and of all our air and sea forces unscathed, so far as the public knew or could be told.
>
> The news astonished the public who could not understand what appeared to be German mastery of the English Channel.
>
> It is certainly not strange that public confidence in the Administration and its conduct of the war should have quavered.

He announced that an inquiry would be held immediately.

In informed naval circles the passage of the ships was not regarded as a defeat. It was considered that while at Brest the enemy ships had tied up our forces at sea to the extent that the Home Fleet had been reduced to one battleship. Now the convoy routes had been relieved of the Brest danger, "Force H" could return to Gibraltar, and the Home Fleet could be brought up to strength to lie at Scapa Flow, from where it could bottle up not only *Tirpitz* but the battle cruisers in their own waters.

The Prime Minister reflected these views in a letter to President Roosevelt aimed at calming the astonishment with which the American people had reacted.

"The naval situation in home waters and in the Atlantic," he wrote, "has been definitely eased by the retreat of the naval forces from Brest. From there they threatened all our Eastbound convoys enforcing a constant two-battleship escort. Our bomber effort can now be concentrated on Germany."

Roosevelt accepted this argument and a cabled reply said:

"When I speak on the radio next Monday evening I shall say a few words to those people who treat the episode in the Channel as a defeat. I am more and more convinced that the location of all German ships in German waters makes our North Atlantic naval problem more simple."

Meanwhile, the German naval authorities had not lost the import of their "retreat". The Naval War Diary said:

> A deep impression has been made on British public opinion. That it was possible for a group of enemy battleships to sail up the Channel in broad daylight without being stopped by the Royal Navy or Royal Air Force, was a serious blow to faith in British mastery of the sea and air, and above all in the co-operation between the two Services.
>
> At the same time the unfavourable effect of withdrawal from Brest on our strategic position in the North Atlantic began to make itself felt. Within a few days we received news that the British battleships had been withdrawn from the North Atlantic convoy service and were assembled in the north of Scotland.
>
> And Prime Minister Churchill announced in the House of Commons — and this was not only propaganda — that the departure of the German ships from the Atlantic coast had relieved the Admiralty of an incubus which had been threatening them for months.
>
> The Channel dash has shown that such an operation can succeed if it is so unexpected that it can stun the enemy into inactivity or panic, as occurred in the wild throwing in of the first naval and air forces.
>
> But there is no justification for the conclusion that earlier lessons of naval warfare are superseded and that repetition of

the same operation would prove successful. The essential point — surprise — would be lacking.

In that way the Channel dash will remain a unique operation.

Even from a tactical standpoint, the Admiralty thought the British public was reacting with rather more fervour than necessary. It was argued that the occasional passage of enemy units was always a possibility under cover of darkness and in short visibility.

This was a thin argument indeed when compared with the daylight passage of a marked force whose whereabouts had been known for many months and whose intention to pass up Channel had been clearly indicated. The Board of Inquiry was the one way an answer could be found to Churchill's simple reply to the First Sea Lord: "Why?"

CHAPTER 14: THE BOARD OF INQUIRY

The findings of the Board of Inquiry were handed to the Prime Minister at the beginning of March, 1942. For security reasons these could not be published at the time; nor were Members of Parliament permitted to have more than the unhelpful scraps proffered during secret sessions. The turbulence of public anger would eventually die, until, so it was thought, the incident would be swamped by greater and more happy events as the war was fought to ultimate victory.

The lesson of Singapore was forgotten. That this disaster, which was so important in the grand strategy of war, had failed to detract from the nation's shock at the Channel Dash escaped the Government's advisers. Instead of dying, the Channel Dash became an incisive cut, scarred into the emotions of a humiliated generation which would be the last to experience from boyhood to manhood "pride in Britain's power at sea".

That one day of war tore a page from history and destroyed the legends of invincibility which had grown around the Navy since Drake had scuppered the Spaniards in the Dover Straits and Nelson had frustrated the invasion aspirations of Napoleon by preserving English supremacy in the Channel.

The Channel Dash has survived as the subject of bitter controversy throughout the country and particularly in Service circles. It was to prevent this and to allay the fearful alarm at the time that the Board of Inquiry had been convened. It had the opportunity to produce findings which would justify or condemn the actions of responsible leaders who had participated in the British action. In this it failed.

On March 18th Mr Clement Attlee, the Deputy Prime Minister, reported to the Commons that the Bucknill Report had been received and studied. After explaining that the contents could not be disclosed because they might be of value to the enemy, he announced:

> *The general findings do not reveal that there were any serious deficiencies in either foresight, co-operation or organisation between the Services concerned and their respective commands.*

There had been foresight in plenty, ten months of it; but there was such precious little co-ordination that Ciliax could say we had thrown in our forces without plan. Nor would one consider from the Deputy Premier's smug-sounding statement that an entire enemy battle fleet had sailed through the English Channel with seeming impunity.

And it conflicts with the present-day sermon on the role of torpedo bombers in future wars preached at NATO staff courses — that the German Navy's Channel dash was a model of inter-Service planning, while the British "Operation Fuller" was a classic example of befuddled tactical thinking, poor cooperation and almost non-existent co-ordination.

In fairness to the Board of Inquiry it must be assumed that the members were concerned with not only seeking out faults and rebuking the dilettantes, but with maintaining the apparent face of unity in spite of defeat. It is possible that the same Board investigating the same battle today might lean further towards the NATO view.

The findings were not only lenient but in some cases difficult to understand. It is, of course, a platitude that to be wise after the event is the pastime of the ignorant; it is equally true that the fringes of fiction can be cut from history only by the most careful analysis. It is upon analysis therefore that the final verdict of the Channel Dash can be pronounced.

Intelligence sources were never revealed by the agencies responsible for them, so the Board was unaware of the activities of the dockyard fitter and other agents to which the planners had been given access. It dealt first with the submarine "iron ring" generally supposed to have existed outside Brest.

Vice-Admiral Binney hoped to persuade the Admiral Commanding Submarines, Admiral Sir Max Horton, to give evidence before the Board on this question, but Sir Max's views on inquiries of any kind not held by himself were notorious.

"If something goes wrong in my Command," he had been known to say, "and I can't damn well find out what it is without setting up a panel of so-called experts, then I'll resign from the Navy and raise chickens." In his report he implied similar sentiments.

Sir Max's staff laid evidence before the Board that *Sealion* was in no way connected with "Fuller"; that she was sent to the Iroise by Sir Max, who hoped that if the big ships were exercising there she might get a chance to attack; that if she had seen the ships break out she would have broken wireless silence to make an enemy sighting report; and that she was the only submarine available for this type of operation.

The remainder of the submarine force was operating in the Mediterranean and in Norwegian waters and two elderly submarines were given patrol areas in the Bay of Biscay to intercept the enemy ships should they break southwards towards the Mediterranean. For these reasons it had not been possible to sustain the effort required to maintain an "iron ring", which had been largely a myth.

Rightly, it seems, the Board was not entirely satisfied that Sir Max had made sufficient sacrifices in other theatres to meet the emergency created by a possible breakout of the Brest ships during February.

It is, of course, very possible that he was acutely conscious of the need for more submarines to replace the heavy losses his Command was suffering in the Mediterranean and on no account would risk his slender reserves in the Channel, which was littered with wrecks, rocks, sandbanks and mines. From the subsequent report of the Board, it appears that this letter ended all attempts to inquire further into the legend of the "iron ring".

Why had we failed to detect the German battle fleet during the fourteen hours it had been at sea before reaching Boulogne? In an effort to find the answer to this question the Board called witnesses concerned with the main Coastal Command reconnaissance patrols — "Stopper", "Line SE" and "Habo".

Coastal Command's formal report on these patrols ignored the alarming gaps in the first, the failure to replace another and the curtailment of the third. No attempt was made to explain the oddities of that night and perhaps it is just as well. It is not pleasant to dwell upon the fact that a blown fuse and a damp plug cheated us of possible victory.

Sir Philip Joubert did, however, complain that "the enemy broke out of Brest unobserved owing to the darkness of the night and the breakdown of radar".

It would appear wholly unnecessary to mention that if he expected the enemy to make his dash in February — as his appreciation of the 8th accurately forecast — then he might also have expected the nights to be black and the weather to be anything but good. Even the most junior officers knew too well that radar of that nature was not wholly effective in those days. And the trained operators had been sent to the Mediterranean leaving only semi-trained crews at home.

The failure to maintain the "Line SE" patrol was an important key to German success. It would have been almost impossible for that patrol to miss the enemy. But someone, somewhere, had not seen fit to plug the most vital gap in the patrols.

The Command's comment on the eventual sighting of the enemy stated:

> The enemy was picked up by normal fighter patrols in time for him to be attacked in the area in which it was originally anticipated that such a course would be possible. To this extent the organisation prepared beforehand worked satisfactorily.

Then, in utter contradiction, the next paragraph said:

> Owing to the short warning obtained... the attack was not so well co-ordinated as might have been the case and no attack could be delivered south of the Dover Straits.

Confronted with this report, the Board scolded the Command mildly for failing to balance the breakdown of the night-patrol organisation with a daylight reconnaissance down the Channel to see if the enemy ships could be detected.

Radar jamming foiled our attempts to pick up the enemy once he entered effective range. For an hour and a half there were radar plots available of enemy aircraft circling over ships in the Channel. Wing Commander Jarvis, Filter Room controller at

Fighter Command headquarters, said in his report:

> I had an instinct backed up by radar tracks that something of import was taking place... and asked on three occasions whether reconnaissances were being sent out to the area concerned.

His efforts to persuade Fighter Command and No11 Group to take action were hardly supported by information from the coastal radar stations at Newhaven, which might well have detected the enemy had they recognised the "atmospheric interference" as deliberate jamming.

The Senior Naval Officer reported to the Admiralty:

> The fact that none of the Newhaven group of stations picked up these targets caused concern and inquiries revealed that all had been subjected to deliberate jamming.
>
> The disturbing point is that it was not treated sufficiently seriously by the personnel concerned to make it the subject of a special report. We had always thought that in the event of a special operation the enemy would jam us. He has done so effectively before.
>
> Had this jamming been reported we would have known that something special was taking place in the Channel and all authorities would have been warned and No11 Group asked for special reconnaissance as a matter of urgency.
>
> Two valuable hours at least would have been gained had this been done. There had been some activity during the night and stations should have been very much on the alert.

This pithy report resolved the breakdown in the radar screen across the Channel. It is more than likely that because there had been plenty of radar activities during the night, the Canadian Army operators were tired. In any event, the human element entered into this side of the picture to the extent that all of two hours were lost.

The Board was concerned with the vitally important question which arose from Beamish's sighting of the enemy and failure to use his wireless to warn Fighter Command. This had led to a delay of half an hour.

The Navy has always employed a system of "sighting reports" whereby, in plain language or code, it is the duty of a ship in contact with the enemy to provide constant information concerning the position, course and speed of the targets to be engaged. The idea of spotting an enemy and then waiting until return to port before telling anyone was not only incredible to Binney, but even, as he remarked to a friend later — "damn stupid".

It would seem that Group Captain Beamish had maintained wireless silence not only because he was obeying orders by doing so, but also because he knew from experience the consequences of breaking it. However, he had been handed the opportunity to warn all England and had failed to grasp it. Why had he not shouted the codeword "Fuller" over R/T?

Both he and Boyd were being chased by enemy fighters. Under such conditions it is hardly likely that a pilot will ponder for long on the problem of disobeying orders. He will be fully occupied with the task of staying alive. Yet a flick of a switch, a shout and half an hour would have been saved.

It is hard to reconcile this with the Board's view that Beamish made the right decision. If both pilots had been shot down, the enemy would have continued his passage undisturbed. And despite Beamish's brilliance as a fighter pilot the possibility of his defeat in the air was not to be ignored. A little more than a month later he died when his Spitfire was shot down over Calais.

No11 Group of Fighter Command were dealt with severely by the Board. The Bucknill Report says:

> The comment we have to make on this question is that unfortunately No11 Group, who were responsible for the "Jim Crow" reconnaissance, were not sufficiently alive to the fact that the German ships might be coming out about that time. True, they knew that Executive Fuller was in operation but some of the witnesses said they had not been informed that there had been any breakdown in the night patrols, and in consequence their minds were not especially directed to the possible significance of the radar plots; and they were slow to order investigation by additional reconnaissance.
>
> Had, however, these plots been investigated as soon as their character came under suspicion, it is possible that the enemy squadron would have been sighted an appreciable time earlier than it was.

This is really a polite way of saying that if No11 Group had been wide awake they might well have saved two hours — during the finer weather when Bomber Command could have attacked with armour-piercing bombs.

It seems inexcusable that with "Executive Fuller" in operation and all concerned supposedly keyed up and waiting for the Channel dash, No11 Group could still produce witnesses whose "minds were note specially directed" to the possible significance of the radar plots. The Bucknill Report, which at best only brushes the various authorities with the gentle caress of criticism, makes no mention of this obvious fault.

Fighter Command's major object was to bring the Luftwaffe to battle as well as protect the bombers. Lord Trenchard laid it down as a principle that close escort of bombers is impracticable — only general cover to the area. Yet attempts were made to give battle and provide close escorts with neither coming off quite as favourably as the Command would have liked.

The telling report from Constable-Roberts, which indicated No11 Group as having said they had supplied fighter escort when Esmonde had taken off, was supported by the official report of his assistant at Dover, Flight-Lieutenant G. A. Kidd. This report said that Lieutenant Kidd had tried to keep in touch with both the Swordfish and the fighter escort once they had taken off. Manston told him that the Swordfish had taken off and were circling the airfield, while Hornchurch reported that their fighters were over Manston at the same time.

He pressed for further information and was told that there was no sign of the Swordfish. He asked to speak to the Hornchurch controller, but was told he was busy on the plotting table. Kidd asked the WAAF on the end of the line at Hornchurch to check with the controller as to where the Swordfish were. She replied that the controller said he did not know.

Kidd persisted. The controller should be informed that from the plots given him it was likely that they were too far to the west. The ships were possibly further on. Finally, Kidd was informed that the fighters had failed to join the Swordfish.

He felt deeply and personally concerned. Had he known from Hornchurch that the fighters were going to be late he would have done all he possibly could to keep the Swordfish orbiting. However, Hornchurch were certain that the rendezvous had been made.

The Bucknill Report virtually ignores these reports, yet it was on the strength of information received by his air liaison officers that Admiral Ramsay permitted Esmonde to make his own decision.

There were probably excellent reasons why the fighters could not get away in time; but there is no apparent reason for No11 Group not keeping Esmonde or Manston fully informed on the delays.

By leaving Esmonde in ignorance of the whereabouts of his escort, the Group placed the destinies of seventeen young Fleet Air Arm officers and men in his hands. They would not have had it otherwise, but the question remains grimly alive — should it have happened that way?

In his Bomber Command report Sir Richard Peirse complained bitterly about the weather which would, he thought that morning, preclude operations against the enemy.

By implication, then, the Bomber Command attacks must have been extremely spontaneous and hardly carried out in accordance with any set plan. Apparently, it really expected the torpedo bombers, MTBs and destroyers, to do the job.

Key to the Command's operations was the reduction of the state of readiness. The Board said curtly:

> The evidence placed before us on this matter was not clear, and it may be that the Air Ministry will think it proper to make a further inquiry about it.

This was a clear invitation to the Air Ministry to hold an internal inquiry into the operations of the Command. It would seem logical that the recommendation of a judicial Board backed by the authority of the Inspector-General of the RAF would have been enough to make the Air Ministry fall over itself in haste to set up such an inquiry. But, no! The British side of the Channel Dash is liberally sprinkled with obvious spasms of neglect and it seems that this spread up as far as the

Ministry. For there is no record of any such inquiry ever having been held. It was left to the Board to describe the Command's role as "comparatively ineffective, if gallant".

It is unfortunately apparent that whereas the enemy flew bomber sorties against our meagre destroyer forces until late afternoon, there are excuses only from our side. The reason: as Hitler had foreseen, we could not "conceive and execute lightning decisions". Instead, Bomber Command complained that operations were limited because there had not been "reasonable notice".[16]

The report of Admiral Ramsay was brutally honest. It reflected bitterness at his own failure to anticipate more accurately the enemy's time of arrival in the Straits and at his Command's failure to inflict greater damage on the battle cruisers. With obvious feeling he angrily criticised No11 Group for permitting Esmonde to attack without escort.

This was a direct challenge to the Air Force. Reflecting the opinions of one of the war's outstanding naval leaders, the bitterness shown towards Fighter Command, the barb at Coastal Command's failure to sight the enemy and the caustic rebuke to Bomber Command are only thinly veiled. His own failures are frankly admitted. It was probably felt that, in the interests of unity, reports like Ramsay's should be seen and heard only in the strictest privacy. For no mention of it appears in any published records of the Inquiry.

While considering the reports of Admiral Ramsay, the Board was faced with the question of whether "there was any lack of

---

[16] One view, supported by many officers, for the Command's failure that day is that our heavy bombers, conditioned as they were for planned operations against static land targets, were not trained for short notice strikes on naval forces moving at high speed. If this is accepted, then Hitler was right.

contact between the Services and Commands concerned as to prior organisation for a concerted attack". This was important. If the weak forces of "Fuller" were to be effective, their employment had to be carefully co-ordinated. At the same time there can be too much co-ordination in what can be pre-supposed as a "running battle".

There may have been some misgivings about this, but the Board had decided to avoid hair-splitting by accepting that the maximum possible co-ordination had been achieved. Then Admiral Binney decided to write to Ramsay asking for details of the arrangements for co-operation between Dover Command and the RAF as called for in "Fuller".

Ramsay's reply set alight the fuse of angry discussion and exploded the theory of planned co-ordination.

It condemned those who had planned for ten months and only confided in the Naval Commander of the most vitally affected area a week before the battle.

In summing up, the Board came to grips with the overriding cause of "Fuller's" failure. "It is doubtful," says the Report, "that the forces employed... were sufficient to cripple the battle cruisers."

In effect, then, the Royal Navy and RAF were unable in 1942 to prevent an enemy battle fleet using the English Channel.

The Admiralty's reasons for employing such weak forces were given as:

At the time we had a very weak concentration of sea power stretching from guarding the *Tirpitz*, then waiting to break out from Trondheim, to guarding east-bound convoys against a breakout by the Brest ships. To do this we had the battleships *King George V*, *Rodney* and *Renown*. *Rodney* was in a sad state and needed a refit; *Renown* was at the Clyde to cover an important convoy sailing for the Middle East which would pass Brest. This left only *King George V* to cover *Tirpitz*.

In addition, if we had wished to bring *King George V* down to the Channel it would have invited the whole German air force to have a go.

This is a sorry argument; it lacks substance and is discredited by the enemy's boldness. There was no need to bring *King George V* as far south as the Channel. Grimsby would have been far enough. Neither was there any need to maintain her at such a port indefinitely. The danger period was between the 10th and 15th; and Sir Philip had taken the risk of ordering his Leuchars squadron south inside that period. It is unlikely that a battleship based for five days at a suitable east-coast port, from where she could sail to intercept a Channel dash force, would have been indefensible.

Further, if *King George V* was too valuable a ship to risk, then *Rodney*, despite her "sad state", would have provided an excellent and expendable challenge to the enemy.

But it is in the fear of inviting the German Air Force to attack that the Admiralty can be most heavily censured. For such an invitation would have been far less a risk than the invitation extended to the RAF by the German heavy ships. With impudence and a detailed plan, they had dared to cross our threshold while the Royal Navy recoiled at sending a battleship nearer to the enemy shores than the Scottish ports.

The truth lies in the unexpectedly recalcitrant attitude of the First Sea Lord, Admiral Sir Dudley Pound. A first-class commander, and one of the Navy's better Commanders-in-Chief, he revealed a stubborn reluctance to employ his battleships in any but the safest waters.

When Sir Philip Joubert had suggested to Admiral Power that the Home Fleet should come south for the emergency period, the reply had been:

"No, it can't be done. The First Sea Lord has insisted time and time again that he will not permit capital ships to operate in the south, where they will be exposed to the dangers of air assault, mines and difficult navigational waters."

There is more sense in the RAF's excuse for not having sufficient strength. Coastal Command's main torpedo force was employed in the Middle East — then considered our major theatre of operations. Its flying strength in Britain had been reduced to the lowest operational safety margin — two and a half squadrons. A breakout from Brest or a dash from Trondheim by *Tirpitz* would call for torpedo fire power; the Command never considered itself capable of proving decisive in either event.

Yet it was the most effective striking force on February 12th; and its efficiency suffered from the human element, which intervened sometimes disastrously, and from the lack of torpedo bombing training which affected some attacks.

For a considerable time the crews in England had been engaged solely on "skip" bombing of enemy ships — low-level attacks with bombs aimed to hit the water short of the target and bounce against its side, a state of training that led to the Bucknill Report saying:

> There is no doubt that the well-timed delivery of synchronised attacks by torpedo bombers is an operation which demands a very high standard of training and efficiency, a standard which the Board realises is difficult to attain in time of war.
>
> The Board venture to express the view that against fast, heavily armoured ships the most effective air weapon

available at present is undoubtedly the torpedo-bomber…. The need for the development of a powerful and highly-trained striking force of torpedo bombers seems to be one which calls for urgent consideration.

This recommendation, in itself a sad commentary on the state of the "Fuller" forces, sparked off a bitter controversy which rages today even more fiercely than during the war — should the Fleet Air Arm absorb Coastal Command?

If the German Channel dash of February 12th can be quoted as an example, then there is no argument. Esmonde's Swordfish were the first planes in the air and the only force to attack as a unit. Another three hours elapsed before Coastal Command contacted the enemy and attacked haphazardly in bits and pieces. The Fleet Air Arm won the right that day to claim that the only fully efficient torpedo bomber squadron in the air was 825 Squadron.

Yet the Fleet Air Arm must also answer the vital question which arises from Sub-Lieutenant Lee's assertion to me that at least twenty-four Swordfish remained idle that day at Lee-on-Solent. Why were they not flown to attack? Despite unfortunate incidents, Coastal Command did manage to put every available aircraft into the air, pulling squadrons from as far afield as Scotland and Cornwall into the battle.

The official explanation is that none of the Swordfish crews at Lee-on-Solent was trained — not one pilot, observer or gunner. This is a typical blanket type of "reason why", often put out by all Services. It leaves room for speculation as to whether, perhaps, one, two or three crews could not have been found to reinforce Esmonde.

The Board made no attempt to criticise the view that the enemy would pass through the Dover Straits during darkness.

It was content with: "The probability that the enemy would pass in the dark hours coloured all the actions of Coastal Command and the Admiralty and influenced arrangements made for the patrols, both as to their design and application."

The Air Ministry's original order, which discussed a daylight passage through the Straits as a possibility but not as a probability, was only briefly mentioned. Why was a daylight passage not regarded as probable?

Laymen in military matters have always understood that when planning a major action the authorities concerned invariably take into account all probable eventualities. A daylight passage was at no time given more than a casual glance by the planners of "Fuller", and for some strange reason was totally ignored by Admiral Ramsay.

The Bucknill Report's final dart is directed at the RAF.

> Apart from the weakness of our forces [it said] the main reason for our failure to do more damage to the enemy was the fact that his presence was not detected earlier, and this again was due to the breakdown of the night patrols and omission to send out a strong morning reconnaissance.

While this comment is undoubtedly true, it seems unfair to Coastal and Fighter Commands that they should be singled out in this concluding paragraph by a Board of Inquiry which had supported Beamish's decision to lose half an hour, and ignored entirely the Admiralty's failure to provide enough strength to meet its own proviso — "Only if we can anticipate the plan of their departure can our chances of destroying them be good."

Having said this on February 2nd, and the enemy's plan having been anticipated more or less accurately, the Navy's "chances" were vested in a pitifully tiny force.

Of the RAF, it can be fairly stated that all group commanders departed from Lord Trenchard's principle that close escort of bombers by fighters is not an operation of air warfare. Despite the Air Ministry's intention to bring the Luftwaffe to battle in accordance with this principle, the object was lost in the confusion.

When it reached Service circles the Bucknill Report was received with consternation — not because of what it said, but because of what it implied by omissions. Sir Philip Joubert asserted bluntly that the dispatch of Esmonde's Swordfish was a mistake, that they should have been held back to make a concerted torpedo attack with his own aircraft. On the other hand, the Admiralty were not pleased with Sir Richard Peirse's claim that on the morning of the 12th he had not decided seriously to consider bombing operations. Nor were Their Lordships content — and with some justification — at his reduction in the state of readiness of his bomber force.

The Admiralty were not prepared to let the Beamish sighting report pass without further action, presumably the result of Admiral Binney's later recommendations. An internal memorandum calling for a reversal of policy by Fighter Command said of the two separate fighter patrols:

> The Squadron Leader of the first patrol merely sighted numerous vessels. His sergeant pilot, however, saw a ship with a tripod mast and battleship superstructure. Both pilots of the second patrol definitely identified the battle cruisers. No enemy sighting report was made.
>
> The pilots of the second patrol — both experienced — explained that they were engaged in a dog fight; when they emerged from the fight they were too low to use wireless — yet other evidence said they would have received messages; there was a "certain amount of secrecy about it" and they thought they had better get home quickly to report.

Group Captain Beamish's explanation referred to standing instructions concerning enemy sighting for fighter patrols in the Channel Area and it may be in other areas as well. These instructions forbid the use of wireless and require the aircraft to return to base to report. This principle is sound in normal circumstances since the object of the fighter is to get his report to headquarters without the enemy realising they are being reported.

It seems to the uninitiated, however, that the normal rule should not be applied to enemy warships of the size of cruisers and above.

In these circumstances it is suggested that the question of enemy sighting reports for ships of certain sizes be raised with the Air Ministry.

One month later Fighter Command amended the standing instructions to permit breaking of wireless silence for sightings of warships of destroyer size and above and of convoys of more than twenty ships. It is probable that the Board of Inquiry accepted the Group Captain's actions only because of this inadequate Standing Order.

The significance of the damage sustained by *Gneisenau* while she lay in Brest seems to have escaped the Board of Inquiry. The bombing offensive had been maintained for nearly a year. Four bombs hit *Gneisenau*, five fell on *Scharnhorst* and one on *Prinz Eugen*. The longest period to repair this damage was five months. The really crippling blow was delivered by a lone Coastal Command torpedo bomber which accompanied one night raid and successfully destroyed *Gneisenau*'s stern.

The battle cruiser was immobilised for nearly nine months because of this one torpedo; yet no attempt was made to repeat this form of attack by a squadron of torpedo bombers. The Fleet Air Arm specialised in torpedo attacks on enemy warships and had scored numerous successes in the

Mediterranean. It would seem reasonable for them to have launched a night attack against the Brest ships from Lee-on-Solent which might have destroyed one or more of the enemy ships before they sailed.

The accepted reason for not doing so is that the targets were in drydock most of the time and protected by anti-torpedo booms when out. Was there, then, no opportunity to repeat the torpedo attack? Not all who took part in "Fuller" believe this. They say there must have been times when a torpedo bomber attack might have been successful — particularly in the danger period when, in fact, they were exercising outside Brest. After all, *Sealion* was there to fire torpedoes, so why not aircraft?[17]

The most likely explanation of why this form of attack was never seriously considered is that the Admiralty and Air Ministry were not unduly concerned at the prospect of a Channel dash being successfully accomplished. In their view any move to home waters made by the Brest ships would relieve the pressure on Atlantic convoys, the Mediterranean and the Home Fleet. It would be a withdrawal by the enemy from his position of holding the initiative in the war at sea.

Both Service Departments hoped that the slender forces commanded by Ramsay and Joubert primarily would bring off an unexpected victory; but if they failed, nothing was lost that could not be expended and the overall strategy of the war would be vastly improved. The entire German surface fleet would be in waters where they could be watched and contained.

---

[17] Coastal Command frequently considered torpedo attacks while the enemy lay in Brest, but torpedoes require some distance after dropping to settle. This distance was not available in Brest. Perhaps this consideration also influenced the Fleet Air Arm.

If this was indeed the accepted, but unspoken, belief of the Naval and Air planners, then their expectations were fully realised — and in permitting the enemy all but meagrely disputed passage home, they destroyed the romantic legend of the Royal Navy's supremacy in the English Channel.

However, in spite of the planning cynicism a gleam of partial success was to shine bleakly through the gloom; the despondent mood of the nation was to be lifted lightly. The Channel Dash was not total defeat.

The German battle squadron achieved a sort of victory never before attempted; in doing so they ended their careers as fighting ships. Six months passed before the *Scharnhorst* could sail again. And when she did, the Home Fleet, commanded by Admiral Sir Bruce Fraser,[18] pounced upon her off the North Cape and sent her to the bottom. *Prinz Eugen*, one of the finest ships in the German Navy, was being towed from one repair yard to another in German waters only two weeks after the Channel Dash, when a British submarine fired a torpedo at her, ripping off the stern. She never sailed again during the war. In 1948 she became part of the United States Navy in the Allied share-out of spoils.

The proud *Gneisenau* was so badly damaged by the mine, and in an air raid later carried out by Bomber Command, that she took no further interest in the war. While in drydock her fate was sealed two weeks later, when Bomber Command wrecked her bows and foredecks with repeated hits, thereby completing her destruction. Her rusting hulk was filled with concrete and she became a block-ship fort, her guns turned against an attack which never came.

No, this armada had not come through entirely unscathed, and the sacrifice of Esmonde's life had been salvaged by the

---

18 Now Admiral of the Fleet Lord Fraser.

mine-laying operations of Bomber Command a few days previously.

Colonel Ibel, the Luftwaffe liaison officer aboard *Scharnhorst*, had ended his association with the trip as quickly as possible. "Now I have had enough," he told Admiral Ciliax. "What is my bill for the ride?" And Admiral Raeder, the German Navy's Supreme Commander, was in no mood to rejoice.

"We have won a tactical victory," he announced, "and suffered a strategic defeat."

True words these, but the British man-in-the-street could not be expected to appreciate their subtlety. He looked for tangible victories from the Royal Navy and RAF, not the infliction of "strategic defeats". For in such circumstances it is only the few intimately concerned with grand strategy who can find comfort in thoughts of possible successes in the future. In war, the uninformed majority must judge events as they happen, day by day.

The London national newspaper, *News Chronicle*, summed up our operations in an editorial:

> This story, though one of individual courage and steadfast devotion to duty, is not one which reflects much credit on those primarily responsible.

No matter what the alibis, what the arguments or the excuses and despite the Bucknill Report, the Channel Dash remains a monument to muddled leadership at the top; and a battle roll of honour for the men who fought in dark and light blue uniforms.

It would not be true to assume that Eugene Esmonde died in vain or without purpose; nor did the sailor-airmen who followed him, the four who perished in the indomitable little *Worcester* or the many pilots and crews of Fighter, Bomber and

Coastal Commands who failed to return. Their purpose was to accomplish the victory regarded by the Admiralty and Air Ministry as unlikely. That they failed in no way diminished their valour.

Failure, even with honour, says an official record, is a melancholy word; but success is not always the full measure of glory. There are so-called failures which will live in history when victories are forgotten. The Charge of the Light Brigade at Balaclava was one of them. The gallant sortie of Eugene Esmonde and his six Swordfish was another.

EPILOGUE

While the repercussions of the Channel Dash rumbled round Whitehall the nation roused itself from the shock to acclaim the personal sacrifice of the man who had chosen duty at the cost of his life. The *London Gazette* announced that the King had awarded the Victoria Cross posthumously to Eugene Esmonde, an honour reflecting the glory of all who died that day, symbolised in the person of the Irishman.

The citation, acknowledged by many as the most moving of them all, read:

> Lieutenant-Commander Esmonde knew well that his enterprise was desperate. Soon after noon he and his squadron of Swordfish set course for the enemy and after ten minutes' flight were attacked by a strong force of enemy fighters. Touch was lost with his fighter escort and in the action which followed all his aircraft were damaged. He flew on cool and resolute, serenely challenging hopeless odds, to encounter the deadly fire of the battle cruisers and their escorts which shattered the port wing of his aircraft.
>
> Undismayed, he led his squadron on, straight through this inferno of fire, in steady flight towards their target. Almost at once he was shot down, but his squadron went on to launch a gallant attack... from which not one of them returned.
>
> His high courage and splendid resolution will live in the traditions of the Royal Navy and remain for many generations a fine and stirring memory.[19]

---

[19] Esmonde was the seventh Irishman and fifth Roman Catholic to win the VC.

To the three Esmonde brothers serving in the Forces — Witham in the Navy, Patrick in the RAMC and Owen in the RAF — no person other than their mother could possibly receive this high award on behalf of the family. At Drominagh, where she was stricken with arthritis, Mrs Esmonde spent more and more time in the wheel-chair bought for her by Eugene. It would be difficult for her to make the long trip from Tipperary.

Captain Patrick Esmonde was stationed in England and most conveniently placed to cut through red tape and organise his mother's journey from Drominagh to Buckingham Palace. He wrote at the time:

"When the news that Eugene had been awarded the VC came over the wireless I was at Penzance and I listened that night to as magnificent a tribute as I have ever heard paid to anyone by the BBC. I thought of Mother at Drominagh, of the immeasurable consolation this must bring her in her great sorrow and then I thought that if it was the last thing I ever did, and if only Mother was willing, I would ensure that she should receive this great reward from the King himself."

On March 1st Paddy arrived in London and drove to the Admiralty, where he saw the Duty Commander. He was directed to the proper department and there "found a Miss Watts and placed my hopes before her. I insisted that if my mother would agree she must receive this award."

He explained that his mother was an invalid and lived in Tipperary; this meant, he added somewhat anxiously, she would need an aeroplane. Miss Watts proved herself of that somewhat rare breed of civil servant who understand the feelings of ordinary people. She took charge of Paddy's problem, promised to try to arrange suitable transport and brusquely instructed him to secure his mother's agreement at once. The next day Paddy arrived in Dublin, where he was joined by his sister, Carmel. On the 3rd they drove to Drominagh together.

Mrs Esmonde was persuaded over lunch, and in the afternoon they set off again for Dublin. In the evening he telephoned Miss Watts at the Admiralty and heard the news that the Fifth Sea Lord had agreed to place a Fleet Air Arm aircraft at Mrs Esmonde's disposal — this is the only known time in the war when a naval aircraft was assigned to a civilian unconnected with military or political operations. During the next week Paddy spoke to Miss Watts on the telephone almost daily from Dublin, planning the details of the trip.

It was no coincidence, but at the King's command, that this particular investiture was to be held on March 17th, St Patrick's Day. It was also by special arrangement at the Admiralty, presumably by the indefatigable Miss Watts, that the Fifth Sea Lord's personal plane, a Dominic, was to be used.

Paddy returned to London on the 9th to complete his plans. Here he learned that the Admiral's Dominic was in Scotland, but would pick him up on the 14th at Chester for the flight across to Belfast. It was to be piloted by an old Fleet Air Arm friend of Eugene's, Lieutenant-Commander Sir George Lewis.

Despite bad weather, Sir George reached Chester as arranged, picked up Paddy and set off for Northern Ireland. The weather worsened and they made a forced landing at the Isle of Man. After an hour they were able to take off again. Over Belfast they were informed by wireless that the city was under an air-raid alert, that balloons were up — visibility was so bad they could not see them — and that they should land at another field 20 miles to the north.

The Dominic landed in the early evening and, after borrowing civilian clothes, the two officers caught a train to

Dublin. It was Sir George's first visit to neutral Dublin and he made the most of it that night. With only one day to go before the Investiture, Paddy was obsessed by the weather — for only the weather could spoil his mother's chances of reaching the Palace.

The next morning Sir George caught an early train back to Belfast to see that his aircraft was serviced for the return trip. Meanwhile Paddy drove in a car loaned by the British Legation to pick up his mother and sister.

They reached Belfast shortly after noon and another special car raced them north to the emergency airfield where Sir George waited alongside the aircraft. Fortunately, the Dominic's door was wide enough to enable Mrs Esmonde to climb aboard with comparative ease. The wheel-chair remained behind.

The weather was appalling, and the visibility low. Despite all the protests of the RAF officers present, Sir George insisted he must take off. In the record of the trip, Paddy wrote:

> So we took off on the 16th at 1pm — Mother, Carmel and myself with Sir George piloting with a crew of two. It was very bumpy and we could hardly see the ends of the wings. My eyes were, of course, on Mother. How was she going to react to this very unpleasant flight? This, coupled with the thought that George might turn back at any moment, gave me plenty to think about.
>
> I soon discovered that Mother was by far the least concerned of the six of us in that plane; and that George, having set course for England, intended staying on it. So we plodded onwards and eventually at three o'clock landed at Chester. At any rate we had Mother in England, even though it was the wrong place. Then George decided to fly on, low through the valleys, to London.

Once again he made it successfully through very bad weather and we landed at Hendon at five. A magnificent car drew up alongside the plane — the Fifth Sea Lord's personal car. By six o'clock we were in London drinking tea at the Welbeck Hotel. Mother had taken the long journey from neutral Ireland wonderfully and seemed quite surprised when everyone asked her if she was tired.

By this time Owen Esmonde had joined the family party, all of whom went to bed early that night in preparation for the momentous morning ahead. Paddy's record continued:

Owen and I took Mother to Buckingham Palace at 10 am. All three of us wore shamrock. Though I have no hope of describing adequately the incredible beauty of the next hour I shall attempt to draw a picture of the most glorious morning of my life.

It was a definite rule that only two people at a time will go before the King; and we were three strong. A policeman tried to stop us at the gates to the Palace, but this was very soon put right when he heard who we were. Then we went up through the courtyard to the front door. I got out and told a sergeant of the Palace Home Guard who we were — and at once a bath chair was miraculously produced.

Mother was carried into the Palace by Owen and myself helped by two Home Guards and we found ourselves in a magnificent long hall filled with chairs. Already, many people had arrived. We were put in the front row, as Mother was to be the first to go up. A Major of Marines came up and spoke to Mother, saying he regretted that only one of us would be allowed to go up with her. After hearing the circumstances, he volunteered to ask the King if we could both accompany Mother. This he did and the King apparently agreed, for we were told by the Major that both of us could go with Mother.

This was entirely an investiture for next-of-kin and I suppose there were about 200 people representing a hundred heroes. There were mothers, wives, sweethearts and quite a number of children. Next to us was a Senior Army Chaplain and his VAD daughter, there to receive his son's George Cross — a Wing Commander who had been killed in Malta. Amongst those 200 people I never saw one cry. All looked serious and sad and I felt there was an immense atmosphere of pride in that Hall. It was a wonderful and thrilling experience to be sitting with those people.

At about 10.30 an Admiral who had already spoken once to Mother gave us a short talk on Procedure — I am nearly sure he was Evans of the *Broke*. Now we were all in rows along the length of this magnificent Hall, and facing us in the centre was a large door. It was through this door that the King had to enter at eleven o'clock.

As Mother was to be the first up, we were told to wheel her in her chair to about ten yards from this door so that she would be ready as soon as the King came in. Owen pushed the right-hand side and I the left. When the King entered, everyone stood. This was indeed a thrill. I can't tell you how grand he looked. He was dressed in naval uniform and the first thing that struck me was how young he looked and frightfully fit. He told us all to sit down.

It is as well to remember that this was no British or Commonwealth family owing allegiance to the King of England. This was the mother and two sons of a proud, nationalistic Irish family. Paddy's record is probably the more poignant for it.

Flanked by her two sons in uniform, who wheeled her forward, Mrs Esmonde bowed her head before the Monarch who was to hand her his country's highest decoration for valour for another son, who had died wearing a dark blue uniform of the Royal Navy. The brothers stood at attention one pace behind the wheel-chair on either side. It was a tender, proud moment for a family which had fought either for or against England for centuries.

As though aware of the traditions represented by the elderly lady facing him, King George VI bent down to shake her hand. With the sincerity of a man who recognises the well from which a son's courage often springs, he expressed his sorrow at Eugene Esmonde's death, recalling that only recently he had invested him with the DSO. In reply, Mrs Esmonde spoke simply of the great honour it was for her to receive the Victoria Cross on behalf of her son. The King said he had been concerned about her trip across from Ireland and hoped the return journey would prove more comfortable.

And while this briefly delicate exchange took place, the King handed her the open box in which was laid the Victoria Cross. Then he stepped forward, smiled at the two brothers behind the chair and clasped their hands.

Owen and Paddy turned their mother round and wheeled her back behind the rows of chairs, where each in turn kissed the Cross and murmured: "For Eugene."

In the early afternoon they boarded the aircraft again for the first part of the long journey back to Drominagh. The weather was bright and clear. On the banks of Lough Derg the brooding, grey-walled house waited to receive one more symbol of an Esmonde who had done his duty — in the service of England.

The sea is selfish and possessive. It rarely relinquishes its hold on those who sail upon its stormy surface and die in its unyielding embrace. Now and then the grip relaxes, and a victim is recovered.

At the end of April a body kept afloat by a semi-inflated lifebelt was brought up the Thames by the tides and washed ashore on the Kent coast. The dead man wore the uniform of a lieutenant-commander in the Royal Navy, and the gold wings on his left sleeve indicated that he had belonged to the Fleet Air Arm. On the little finger of his left hand was a signet ring.

Coastal defence patrols informed the naval authorities at Chatham, where the body was taken by ambulance. The jacket of the uniform was stained with blood from a line of bullet-holes down the back from neck to waist. Investigations at Lee-on-Solent soon disclosed the identity of the man who wore the signet ring.

The compassionate sea, calm after the angry turbulence over which 825 Squadron had flown on its now historic mission, had delivered up the body of Eugene Esmonde, VC.

POSTSCRIPT

The Bucknill Report was tabled before Parliament as a White Paper in 1946 at a time when Members were more concerned with establishing the Welfare State than with political inquisitions on military incidents. Not so the Services concerned.

The Channel Dash had given birth to the suspicion inside the Air Ministry that the Admiralty were out to "pinch" Coastal Command. A row started up with retiring Admirals and Air Marshals throwing — and dropping — assorted bricks which not only hurt, but astonished those field commanders who had done their best to avert disaster. Two of the latter were Sir Philip Joubert and Admiral Power. In his book *The Third Service*, Joubert says: "It is necessary to show how the inter-Service conflict of today has been nourished by these experiences of the past.... Looking back on the Navy-Coastal Command relationship at the time, I am amazed that out of the friendliness and mutual trust of this period there should have been born the present spirit of rancour."

I have no intention of taking sides in this conflict; nor is this book written to denigrate one Command or Service to the advantage of another. Rather is it intended simply to explain why an operation never before undertaken successfully by an enemy of England should have been possible in 1942.

It is also intended as a tribute to the men who fought, died and survived. As such it would not be worthwhile unless the circumstances surrounding their actions were given in detail.

That this detail would lead to criticisms of some Commands, even individuals, was inevitable. These have been fair criticisms, I hope, made without preference or prejudice. The results show clearly that all concerned did their best; they did it in accordance with British fighting tradition, with too little, too late. This of course, is not the official view, nor do the Admiralty and Air Ministry endorse my comments, which are my own.

Could this futility be repeated today? I say yes, and again yes. Twice now thousands of young men have gone to war and learned to curse politics. They were called up, and the first were indoctrinated with a sense of pride in dying while the muddle was unravelled. Ships sailed early in 1940 without anti-aircraft guns, some without ammunition. The first tormented cry from the Army was: "Where is a tank that can *kill?*" Mitchell, inventor of the Spitfire, became a hero *after* war broke out.

We shall win a future war because, as a race, we are not equipped to lose. How much would we save if our Services were equipped to win — *now*.

The Channel Dash provides a lesson in public relations that the Service Departments might do well to absorb. Beneath a veneer of casual indifference we are an emotional race. We are deeply affected by trivial events even when great occasions are in the offing. The plight of a stranded dog, or a lost child, or of a family unjustly evicted from their home, can arouse us to greater passions than any politically or militarily momentous event in some remote corner of the world.

Thus, in 1942, the undermining of cherished legends of the sea by the Channel Dash caused greater consternation to the uninformed millions than did the fall of Singapore, a bastion thousands of miles away and at the importance of which only a few could guess.

I do not expect the many serving and retired officers and officials who so kindly assisted me in my research to agree with all the criticisms and comments I made in this book. They may concur with some, however, and acknowledge perhaps the validity of most.

Sir Edgar Ludlow-Hewitt, Admiral Sir C. T. Mark Pizey, Sir Philip Joubert, Group Captain Gleave and Edgar Lee, now a schoolmaster in Suffolk, have been particularly kind and generous in their assistance. Mr George Hurford and his staff of the Admiralty Historical Section gave ready help and patiently led me through many pitfalls.

I must acknowledge my debt to HMSO for the use of material contained in the Bucknill Report (Command 6775), and for other official records held in Crown copyright. Although I have had access to certain official records for the purpose of writing this book, I must repeat that the statements made and the views expressed by me are entirely my own.

To the late Mrs Esmonde and Eugene's twin, James, I must express my deep gratitude for permitting me unrestricted use of family documents, thereby providing me with the opportunity to dedicate this book to Eugene Esmonde and the Fleet Air Arm.

A NOTE TO THE READER

If you have enjoyed this book enough to leave a review on **Amazon** and **Goodreads**, then we would be truly grateful.
Sapere Books

Sapere Books is an exciting new publisher of brilliant fiction and popular history.

To find out more about our latest releases and our monthly bargain books visit our website: **saperebooks.com**